MASTERING THE PSSA GRADE 4 SCIENCE TEST

MARK JARRETT

Ph.D., Stanford University

STUART ZIMMER

JAMES KILLORAN

JARRETT PUBLISHING COMPANY

EAST COAST OFFICE
P.O. Box 1460
Ronkonkoma, NY 11779
631-981-4248

SOUTHERN OFFICE
50 Nettles Boulevard
Jensen Beach, FL 34957
800-859-7679

WEST COAST OFFICE
10 Folin Lane
Lafayette, CA 94549
925-906-9742

www.jarrettpub.com
1-800-859-7679   Fax: 631-588-4722

Jarrett Publishing Company
Post Office Box 1460
Ronkonkoma, New York 11779

ISBN 0-9795493-8-8   [978-0-9795493-8-0]
Printed in the United States of America
First Edition
10 9 8 7 6 5 4 3 2   10 09 08

ACKNOWLEDGMENTS

The authors would like to thank the following science educators who helped review the manuscript. Their respective comments, suggestions, and recommendations have proved invaluable in preparing this book.

Keith Butler
Eastern Representative and Membership Chairman
Pennsylvania Science Teachers Association (PSTA)
Biology and Environmental Science Teacher
Emmaus High School
Emmaus, Pennsylvania

Ted Robertson
Environmental Programs Director
Science Education Specialist
Lawrence Hall of Science
University of California
Berkeley, California

Ruth Rudd
President, Pennsylvania Science Teachers Association (PSTA)
Science Consultant and Lecturer, Cleveland State University
Presidential Award for Excellence in Science Teaching

Layout, graphics, and typesetting: Burmar Technical Corporation, Albertson, N.Y.

This book is dedicated…

to my wife, Gośka, and my children Alexander and Julia　　*— Mark Jarrett*

to my wife Joan, my children Todd and Ronald, and
my grandchildren Jared and Katie Rose　　*— Stuart Zimmer*

to my wife Donna, my children Christian, Carrie, and Jesse,
and my grandchildren Aiden, Christian, and Olivia　　*— James Killoran*

TABLE OF CONTENTS

INTRODUCTION

UNIT 1: THE NATURE OF SCIENCE

UNIT 2: SCIENTIFIC INVESTIGATION AND TECHNOLOGY

UNIT 3: BIOLOGICAL SCIENCES

UNIT 4: PHYSICAL SCIENCES

UNIT 5: EARTH AND SPACE SCIENCES

UNIT 6: A PRACTICE PSSA TEST IN SCIENCE

WHAT IS THE PSSA GRADE 4 SCIENCE TEST?

This year, you will take your first PSSA test in science. The **PSSA Grade 4 Science Test** has 62 multiple-choice questions. Each multiple-choice question asks a question and gives four possible answer choices.

Of the 62 multiple-choice questions, only 56 will count. Six questions will be sample questions for future tests. Since you won't know which questions count, do your best on all questions. There's no penalty for guessing a wrong answer. Answer every question even if you are unsure of the answer.

There will also be seven short-answer questions. These questions require you to write a brief response of two or three sentences. Of these, only five questions will count towards your score. Two will be practice questions and do not count.

The questions on the test that do count are divided into the following categories:

CATEGORIES	Multiple Choice	Short-Answer	Total Points
Category 1: The Nature of Science These questions test your understanding of science and scientific investigation. They include designing scientific questions, methods of investigation, measuring, reading graphs and charts, comparing models, and making predictions.	29 or 31	1 or 2	**33**
Category 2: Biological Sciences These questions test your understanding of living things, including plants, animals, inherited characteristics, and ecosystems.	7 or 9	1 or 2	**11**
Category 3: Physical Sciences These questions test your understanding of matter, motion, force, and the different types of energy.	7 or 9	1 or 2	**11**
Category 4: Earth and Space Sciences These questions test your understanding of Pennsylvania's land forms, Earth's resources, the water cycle, the weather, and the movements of Earth, the sun, and the moon.	7 or 9	1 or 2	**11**

As you see, Category 1 has the most questions, since the methods of scientific inquiry and investigation affect almost everything done in science.

HOW CAN THIS BOOK HELP YOU?

Everyone wants to get a high score on the **PSSA Grade 4 Science Test**. But just wanting a high score is not enough. You will really have to work at it. With this book as your guide, you will be much better prepared for the PSSA — and even enjoy studying for it. This book provides a complete "refresher" of all the essential knowledge and skills you will need to do your best.

Students work on a class experiment while taking care to use important safety practices.

This book consists of four units that review and reinforce what you learn in fourth grade science. Each unit has several lessons. Each lesson —

★ opens with a list of *Important Ideas*

★ is divided into small, easy-to-understand sections

★ provides *Applying What You Have Learned* activities to reinforce what you have learned

★ includes *Study Cards* to help you review

★ concludes with *What You Should Know*, which summarizes the main ideas of the lesson

★ provides PSSA-style practice questions, with each one identified by its "Assessment Anchor" and "Eligible Content" standard

You will also find a checklist of the *Grade 4 Science Assessment Anchors* at the end of each unit. Make sure you have mastered each anchor before moving to the next unit. The final part of the book consists of a *complete* practice test, just like the actual **PSSA Grade 4 Science Test**.

HOW TO ANSWER MULTIPLE-CHOICE QUESTIONS

There will be five types of multiple-choice questions on the **PSSA Grade 4 Science Test**. These questions will test your ability to:

| Recall scientific facts, concepts and relationships | Explain or relate scientific facts or events | Explain scientific investigations | Analyze scientific information from graphs, charts, diagrams and maps | Apply scientific concepts |

This lesson will help you to recognize each type of question. You will also learn a method to help you answer each type of question on the test. Let's begin by looking at the first type of question.

RECALLING INFORMATION

Many questions on the test will simply ask you to *recall* or *identify* something you learned in science. For example, examine the question below:

---

1. Which force pulls objects towards Earth?

   A gravity
   B friction
   C magnetism
   D electricity

As you can see, this question tests your ability to recall information about different types of forces.

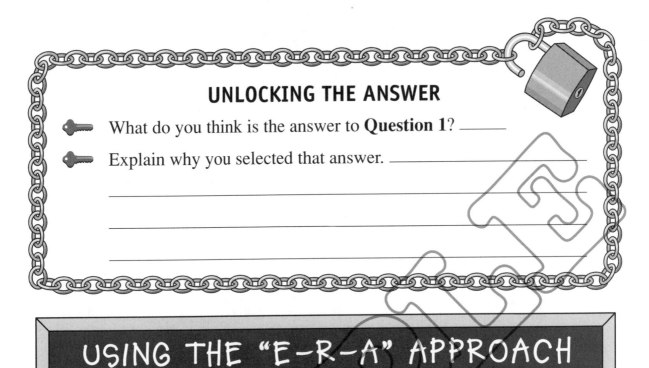

UNLOCKING THE ANSWER

🔑 What do you think is the answer to **Question 1**? _____

🔑 Explain why you selected that answer. _____

_____

_____

_____

USING THE "E-R-A" APPROACH

Whatever type of question you are asked, we suggest you follow the same three-step approach to answer it. Think of this as the "**E-R-A**" approach:

EXAMINE
the question

RECALL
what you know

APPLY
what you know

Let's take a closer look at each of these steps to see how they can help you select the correct answer.

STEP 1: EXAMINE THE QUESTION

Start by reading the question carefully. Make sure you understand any information the question provides. Then make sure you understand what the question is asking for.

HINT

The question on page 3 is asking you to identify (or name) the force that pulls objects to Earth.

STEP 2: RECALL WHAT YOU KNOW

Next, you need to identify the topic of science that the question asks about. Take a moment to think about what you know about that topic. Mentally review the important concepts, facts, and relationships you can remember.

*In this case, you should think about what you can recall from your study of motion and force. The question asks which **force** pulls things to Earth. Sit back and think about what you can recall about this topic.*

★ *You may remember that **gravity** is the name scientists have given to the force of attraction between all objects.*

★ ***Gravity** helps determine the paths of Earth and the moon in space. **Gravity** also causes objects to fall to Earth's surface.*

★ ***Friction** is caused by the rubbing of objects. **Magnetism** is a force that attracts some metals. **Electricity** is a form of energy.*

STEP 3: APPLY WHAT YOU KNOW

Now take what you can recall about the topic and apply it to the question. Often, it helps to try to answer the question on your own **before** you look at the four answer choices. Then, see if any of the answer choices is what you think the answer should be.

Look at all the answer choices carefully to make sure you choose the best one. You should cross out any choices that are obviously wrong.

1. Which force pulls objects towards Earth?

   A gravity
   B friction
   C magnetism
   D electricity

Here, the question asks you to identify which force pulls objects towards Earth. To answer this question, you need to recall the characteristics of different types of forces. Then apply this information to select the force that pulls objects to Earth.

EXPLAINING OR RELATING SCIENTIFIC FACTS OR EVENTS

Some questions on the test may ask you to explain or relate scientific facts or events. These questions go beyond just recalling information. They ask you to use your higher thinking skills. These questions might ask you to:

Compare things

Explain why or how something happened

Give an example of something

Identify the cause or effect of an event

Place events or steps of a process in order

Let's look at a sample question asking you to explain why something happens:

2. What causes the moon to appear to change its shape each month?

   A   Our view of the part of the moon reflecting sunlight changes.
   B   Earth's orbit around the sun changes.
   C   The sun's temperatures increase and decrease each month.
   D   Earth's spinning on its axis reflects light on the moon.

UNLOCKING THE ANSWER

What do you think is the answer to **Question 2**? _____

To help you answer this type of question, you should again apply the "**E-R-A**" approach.

STEP 1: EXAMINE THE QUESTION

Read the question carefully, and be sure you know what it asks for.

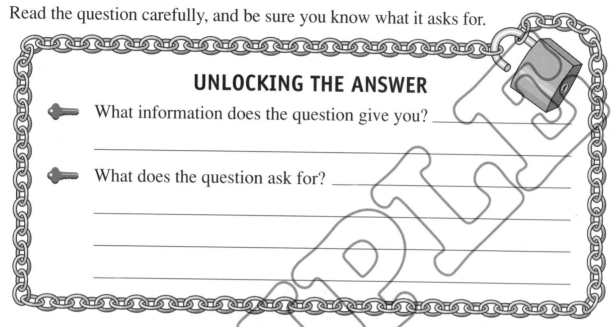

UNLOCKING THE ANSWER

What information does the question give you? _____

_____

What does the question ask for? _____

_____

_____

_____

_____

STEP 2: RECALL WHAT YOU KNOW

Again, you need to identify the science topic the question asks about. Here, the question asks about Earth and Space Sciences. The specific topic it asks about is the moon. Now take a moment to push back your chair and put on your imaginary "thinking cap." Think about what you know about that topic. Review those concepts and facts you can remember about the moon.

UNLOCKING THE ANSWER

What information do you recall about the moon and its

movement? _____

_____

_____

_____

HINT *What do you recall learning about the moon in science class? At night, we see the light that the moon reflects from the sun. Each month, the part of the moon reflecting the sun's light grows until it*

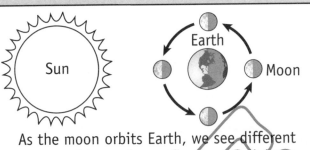

As the moon orbits Earth, we see different parts of its surface reflecting sunlight.

reaches a full moon. It then shrinks again until the moon is entirely dark. The part of the moon that we see reflecting sunlight changes as the moon moves along its orbit.

STEP 3: APPLY WHAT YOU KNOW

Finally, apply what you can recall about the topic to the question. Remember to cross out any choices that you think are obviously wrong. Then carefully look over the remaining answer choices. Be sure to select the best answer.

EXPLAINING SCIENTIFIC INVESTIGATIONS

Some questions on the PSSA will examine your ability to conduct or explain scientific investigations. Here are some of the things you may be asked to do:

Identify what question a scientific investigation is trying to answer	**Select the best tools for a scientific investigation**	**Design or describe procedures for an investigation**
Make scientific measurements	**Identify variables tested in a scientific investigation**	**Make observations or predictions from an investigation**

For example, look at the question below about scientific investigation:

---

4. Which instrument allows scientists to measure air pressure?

    A   thermometer

    B   barometer

    C   beaker

    D   telescope

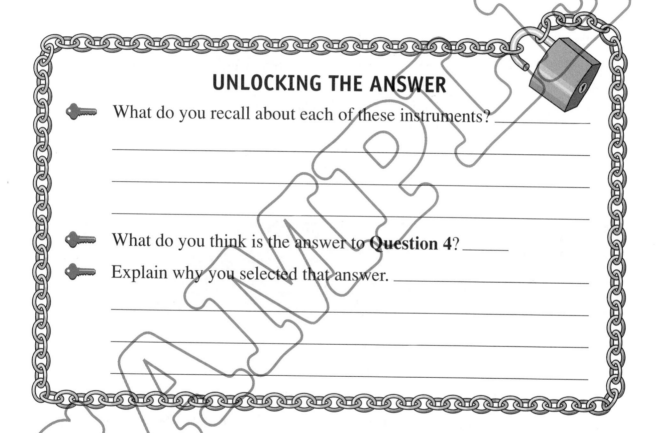

UNLOCKING THE ANSWER

What do you recall about each of these instruments? _____

_____

_____

_____

What do you think is the answer to **Question 4**? _____

Explain why you selected that answer. _____

_____

_____

USING THE "E-R-A" APPROACH

✦ **Step 1: <u>E</u>XAMINE the Question**

First, examine any information in the question. Then determine what the question is asking for.

This question asks you to determine which instrument scientists use to measure air pressure.

USING THE "E-R-A" APPROACH

✦ **Step 2: RECALL What You Know**

Now, identify the topic of the question. Recall what you know about it.

Think about what you can remember about scientific instruments and the weather. You might recall that air pressure is the force created by the weight of the air above the measuring point. You might also remember how scientists measure air pressure.

✦ **Step 3: APPLY What You Know**

Finally, apply your knowledge to the question. Cross out any wrong answer choices. Select the best answer choice remaining.

*If you recall that a **barometer** is used to measure air pressure, then you can answer the question easily. What if you don't remember what a barometer is? You might still be able to select the correct answer. Start by eliminating those choices you know are wrong. You might recall that a thermometer measures temperature. A beaker can be used to measure volume. A telescope observes distant objects. Since none of these measures air pressure, the correct answer must be **Choice B**.*

ANALYZING SCIENTIFIC INFORMATION

A third type of question on the PSSA examines your ability to **analyze scientific information**. To **analyze** means to break something up into its parts.

An analysis question usually presents scientific data or observations in a diagram, table, graph, or map. This type of question will often show the results of a scientific investigation. You will then be asked to do one of the following:

- Summarize, describe or interpret the information
- Explain the information
- Describe patterns or relationships
- Draw conclusions
- Choose the best model to represent the information

Let's look at a sample question asking you to analyze scientific information.

5. Copper wires are connected to a battery and an electric bulb, as shown in Figure 1. The bulb lights up. When one of the wires is cut, as shown in Figure 2, the bulb goes out. Which statement

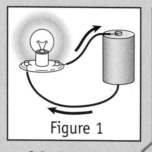

Figure 1

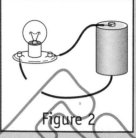

Figure 2

best explains why the bulb in Figure 2 has gone out?

A   The bulb is overheated.

B   Electricity needs a complete circuit to flow.

C   Cutting the wire drains the battery of electricity.

D   Electrical energy changes into light energy.

UNLOCKING THE ANSWER

🗝 How does Figure 2 differ from Figure 1? _____

_____

_____

_____

🗝 What is the answer to **Question 5**? _____

🗝 Explain the reason why you selected your answer. _____

_____

_____

_____

This question presents a brief description with two diagrams. These diagrams show two ways wires can be connected to a battery and a light bulb. In *Figure 1*, the bulb is lit. In *Figure 2*, the bulb has gone out. The question then asks you to explain why the bulb in *Figure 2* has gone out.

How should you answer a question that asks you to analyze scientific information? Again, you should use the "**E-R-A**" approach. Let's see how this approach could be used to answer this question.

USING THE "E-R-A" APPROACH

✦ Step 1: <u>E</u>XAMINE the Question

Read the question carefully. Examine any data or observations it may include. Usually, data will be presented as a diagram, graph, or table. Then determine what the question is specifically asking for.

The data is presented in a brief description with two diagrams. The question asks why the bulb in Figure 2 has gone out. Carefully look over the two diagrams. Think about how the diagrams are different.

✦ Step 2: <u>R</u>ECALL What You Know

Next, take a moment to think about any important facts, concepts or relationships you can recall about the subject of the question.

*You should recognize that the question asks about **electricity**. Think about what you can remember about this topic. You might recall that electricity can create heat and light energy as well as magnetic force. You might also remember that electricity flows in a circuit or path. For electricity to flow in a circuit, the circuit must be complete.*

✦ Step 3: <u>A</u>PPLY What You Know

Apply the information that you remember to select the correct answer. You might first attempt to answer the question without looking at the choices. Then examine the answer choices and eliminate those you know are wrong. Finally, select the best answer from the remaining answer choices.

You should be able to determine that the bulb in Figure 2 goes out because the circuit is incomplete. You should also be able to eliminate some of the wrong answer choices:

★ *Choice C makes no sense. Cutting the wire does not drain the electricity. If the wire were reconnected, the bulb would light up.*

★ *Choice D describes what happens when the wires are connected. As electricity flows through the thin wires in the light bulb, some of this electrical energy changes into light energy. However, this does not explain why the bulb goes out when the wire is cut.*

★ *Choices A and B remain. A bulb could overheat, but not when the wire is cut. Since the wire is cut, the circuit is incomplete. No electricity will flow around the circuit or into the light bulb. **Choice B** is therefore the correct answer.*

APPLYING SCIENTIFIC CONCEPTS

Some questions on the PSSA will ask you to apply scientific concepts to specific situations. These questions will usually ask you to:

Apply your scientific knowledge to new situations

Use scientific concepts to solve problems

Let's look at a sample question that asks you to make connections between scientific concepts and the "real world."

6.   Students often slip on the wet pavement in front of their school when it is raining. How can the school make the pavement less slippery?

   A   make the pavement smoother
   B   wash the pavement with a strong detergent
   C   throw sand and gravel on the pavement
   D   ask students to wear smooth slippers

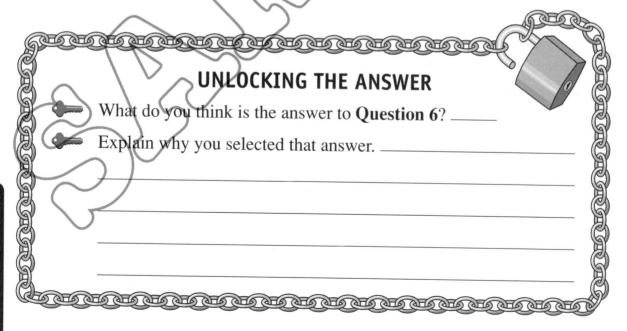

UNLOCKING THE ANSWER

What do you think is the answer to **Question 6**? _____

Explain why you selected that answer. _____

_____

_____

_____

_____

To answer questions asking you to apply scientific concepts to solve a problem, you should again try using the "**E-R-A**" approach:

USING THE "E-R-A" APPROACH

✦ Step 1: <u>E</u>XAMINE the Question

Examine the question carefully. Be sure that you understand the situation or problem presented in the question.

In this question, students are slipping on the wet pavement in front of school. What can the school do to prevent this from happening?

✦ Step 2: <u>R</u>ECALL What You Know

Next, you need to identify those scientific facts, concepts, and relationships that best apply to the situation or problem.

*For this question, you need to recall what you know about the topic of force and motion. What force causes the students to slip? What force could be used to slow down or stop this unwanted motion? You may recall that **friction** acts to reduce motion. Friction increases if the objects rubbing against each other are rough rather than smooth.*

✦ Step 3: <u>A</u>PPLY What You Know

Now use what you know to answer the question. First, think how you might answer the question without looking at the answer choices. Then study the choices carefully, eliminating those that are obviously wrong. Finally, select the best answer.

In this example:

★ *Choice A would make the pavement smoother. This would reduce friction and make the pavement even more slippery.*

★ *Choice B, cleaning the pavement, might also reduce friction. This would make the pavement more slippery.*

★ *Choice D, wearing smooth slippers, would reduce friction and make the pavement even more slippery.*

★ *Choice C is the best answer. Throwing sand and gravel on the wet pavement would make its surface rougher. The pavement would be harder to slip on because of the increased surface friction.*

Now use the "**E-R-A**" approach to answer a second question applying scientific concepts to a "real world" problem.

7. Scientists observe cumulonimbus clouds moving over Philadelphia. What steps should people living in that city take?

   A   get ready for a storm
   B   plan for an earthquake
   C   prepare for sunny weather
   D   expect heavy fog

USING THE "E-R-A" APPROACH

✦ **Step 1: <u>E</u>XAMINE the Question**

What does the question ask you to do? _____

_____

_____

✦ **Step 2: <u>R</u>ECALL What You Know**

What can you recall about this topic? _____

_____

_____

_____

_____

_____

✦ **Step 3: <u>A</u>PPLY What You Know**

Using what you know, how does that help you to find the answer? _____

_____

_____

_____

_____

_____

In this lesson, you learned how to answer different types of multiple-choice questions. In the next lesson, you will learn how to answer short-answer questions.

RESPONDING TO SHORT-ANSWER QUESTIONS

Some questions on the **PSSA Grade 4 Science Test** will require you to write an answer in your own words. The answer sheet will have space for you to write your answer. Each of these short-answer questions is worth 2 points. You may receive no points, 1 point, or 2 points. Your scores will depend on what you write for your answer.

Let's take a look at a sample short-answer question:

1. A rain gauge is one instrument that is used to study changes in weather. A rain gauge measures how much rain has fallen.

> **Part A:** Identify one other instrument that can be used to study the weather.
>
> _____
>
> **Part B:** Describe what the instrument you identified in Part A measures.
>
> _____
>
> _____

SHORT-ANSWER QUESTIONS

There are many ways to approach a short-answer question. One of the best ways is to use these three steps:

Analyze and Plan → Write Your Answer → Review and Revise Your Answer

STEP 1: ANALYZE AND PLAN

When you approach a short-answer question, first look carefully at the directions in the question. The instructions for what you are asked to do will usually be found in the "**action words**" of the question. Here are the most common ones:

Identify	To name something, or to tell what it is.
Describe	To tell what something is like, or how it changes over time.
Explain	To *explain how* something happened, to *explain why it happened* or to *explain its effects*: • To *explain how*, tell the way in which it took place. • To *explain why*, give the reasons why it happened. • To *explain effects*, identify and describe each effect.
Compare	To identify similarities and differences between two or more things.
Predict	To make a statement about what will probably happen in the future
Illustrate	To give examples of something; to draw something.
Measure	To find the length, height, weight, or temperature of something.

After you have studied the "action words" in the question, you should next identify **all** the parts of the question.

USING AN ANSWER BOX

Don't rush into answering the question. Take a few moments to plan your answer. You can do this by simply jotting down some notes you think might be helpful.

It often helps to plan your answer with an **answer box**. This box divides up the different parts of the question. You can either fill in the answer box with your ideas or just check off each part of the box as you answer it.

The answer box serves as a checklist. It makes sure you answer every part of the question. Even if you decide not to write out an answer box, use a "mental answer box" in your head.

Short-answer questions usually have *two* parts. For example, the short-answer question on page 16 asks you to *identify* one instrument used to study the weather. *It then asks you to* **describe** *what this instrument measures.* Here is what a model answer box might look like for this question:

Identify a weather instrument	Your Response
Describe what it measures	Your Response

Look at the next short-answer question. In the space below, create an answer box that could be used to answer the question. You do not have to fill in the boxes for your response. You will learn more about this topic in a later lesson.

2. Human activities often bring changes to the environment.

> **Part A:** Identify one change that human activities have brought to the environment.
>
> _____
>
> **Part B:** Identify a second change that human activities have brought to the environment.
>
> _____

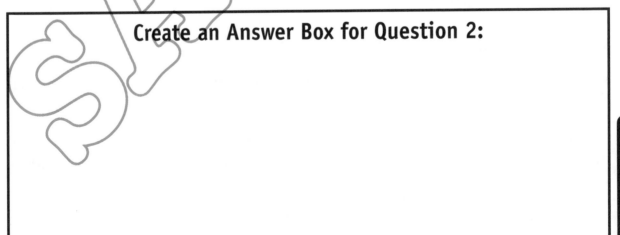

Create an Answer Box for Question 2:

Let's get additional practice creating an **answer box**. Below is a sample short-answer question. Create your answer box in the space provided below.

3. Gravity is one of the forces found on Earth and throughout the universe. It is a force of attraction between any two pieces of matter.

Part A: Identify one other type of force.

_____

Part B: Describe the characteristics of the type of force you identified in part A.

_____

Create an Answer Box for Question 3:

STEP 2: WRITE YOUR ANSWER

The next step in responding to a short-answer question is to *write* your answer.

★ You can use the notes you created in your answer box to write your answer.

★ Turn each point in your notes or answer box into one or more complete sentences. Check off each section of your answer box as you complete it.

STEP 3: REVIEW AND REVISE YOUR ANSWER

The first person to read your answer should be **YOU**—*not* the person scoring it. Once you have finished writing, read over your answer *before* you hand it in.

Make sure you have provided all of the information required by the question. As you review what you have written, ask yourself these questions:

★ Did I follow **all of the directions** in the question?

★ Did I complete **all of the parts** in the question?

★ Did I **provide enough details** to support my answer?

SCORING YOUR ANSWER

To see how your answer will be scored, let's look at a model question.

4. Scientific explanations must be based on facts. Scientists must understand the difference between a fact and an opinion.

> **Part A:** Give an example of a scientific fact. _____
> _____
>
> **Part B:** Give an example of an opinion. _____
> _____

Now let's look at some sample responses written by fourth grade students to this question. Give each student answer a score of "**0**", "**1**," or "**2**."

ANSWER A

> **Part A:** Give an example of a scientific fact. _____
> *Water freezes at 32°F.*
>
> **Part B:** Give an example of an opinion. _____
> *Cold water has a refreshing taste.*

Circle your score:	0	1	2

Explain why you gave that score. _____
_____

ANSWER B

Part A: Give an example of a scientific fact. _____
Horses walk on all four legs.

Part B: Give an example of an opinion. _____
A chicken walks on two legs.

Circle your score: 0   1   2

Explain why you gave that score. _____

_____

_____

_____

_____

ANSWER C

Part A: Give an example of a scientific fact. _____
Americans do not exercise enough.

Part B: Give an example of an opinion. _____
The average American exercises less than 2 hours per week.

Circle your score: 0   1   2

Explain why you gave that score. _____

_____

_____

_____

_____

ANSWER D

> **Part A:** Give an example of a scientific fact. _____
> *After heating a test tube of water for three minutes, the water began*
> *to boil.*
>
> **Part B:** Give an example of an opinion. _____
> *The temperature of the boiling water was 212°F.*

Circle your score: 0   1   2

Explain why you gave that score. _____

_____

_____

_____

_____

Test scorers will use a **rubric**, or scoring guide, to score student responses on the **PSSA Grade 4 Science Test**. The rubric tells a scorer what information needs to be included in the answer to receive a score of **0**, **1**, or **2 points**. Below is a sample rubric for the question you just scored:

Score	In response to this item, the student—
2	demonstrates a thorough understanding of scientific facts and opinions. The response may contain a minor blemish (e.g. misspelled words) or omission that does not take away from demonstrating a thorough understanding. The response is clear, complete and correct.
1	demonstrates a partial understanding of scientific facts and opinions **OR** the response correctly identifies a fact or an opinion but not both.
0	provides insufficient evidence to demonstrate any understanding of a fact or an opinion. Nothing is correct, relevant, or sufficient to earn a score of 1. The response may show only information copied or rephrased from the question, or it may be blank, off-task, or illegible.

Now that you have seen the rubric for scoring responses to this question, would you change any of the scores you gave before?

Which scores would you change and why? _____

_____

_____

_____

Based on the rubric, the answers would probably be scored as follows:

★ **Answer A.** The student correctly identifies one scientific fact and one opinion. Since the response demonstrates a thorough understanding, it should receive a score of **2**.

★ **Answer B.** The student correctly identifies a fact. However, the response that "chickens walk on two legs" is a fact, not an opinion. The student demonstrates only a partial understanding of scientific facts and opinions. Since only one of the two required points is found in this response, it should receive a score of **1**.

★ **Answer C.** The student has mixed up fact and opinion. The student identifies an opinion as a fact, and a fact as an opinion. "Americans do not exercise enough" is an opinion. The statement, "The average American exercises less than 2 hours a week" is a fact. The response fails to demonstrate an understanding of fact and opinion. It should receive a score of **0**.

★ **Answer D.** The student identifies two facts. However, the question asks for one fact and one opinion. The response demonstrates only a partial understanding of fact and opinion. It should receive a score of **1**.

As you can see from this scoring exercise, the length of your answer will not determine the score you receive. The number of lines you write is less important than providing correct information that fully answers the question. The most important part of answering any short-answer question is to:

read the question carefully	answer all parts of the question	use only correct information

UNIT 1 — THE NATURE OF SCIENCE

In this unit, you will look at some basic principles common to all fields of science. To try to understand the natural world, scientists make observations, ask questions, build models, develop scientific explanations and share ideas.

In the next two lessons, you will learn how scientific knowledge develops.

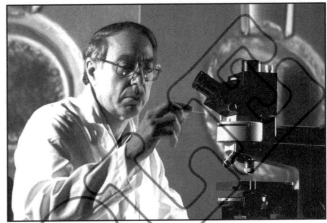

Scientific knowledge is constantly undergoing change.

★ **Lesson 3: What is Science?** In this lesson, you will learn how science first began. You will learn how people observed patterns in nature and asked questions. You will learn that scientific explanations are logical and are based on evidence from observations. You will also learn how scientific explanations are used to make predictions.

★ **Lesson 4: Scientific Reasoning.** In this lesson, you will learn about scientific reasoning and analysis. You will learn the difference between an opinion and a scientific fact. You will learn that a system is a group of things that work together as a whole. Finally, you will also learn that scientists often use models to represent objects or processes.

KEY TERMS YOU WILL LEARN ABOUT IN THIS UNIT

- Patterns
- Cycle
- Science
- Observation
- Scientific Explanation
- Prediction
- Scientific Fact
- Opinion
- Model
- Terrarium
- Systems in Nature
- Human-made Systems

WHAT IS SCIENCE?

In this lesson, you will learn what science is and how it first developed.

— IMPORTANT IDEAS —

A. There are many different patterns in nature.

B. Patterns of repeating events in nature make **predictions** possible.

C. Science attempts to explain what happens in nature. **Scientific explanations** are logical and are based on evidence from **observations**.

D. Scientific explanations can be tested. When an explanation is unable to explain an observation, the explanation must be changed.

E. Scientific explanations can be used to make predictions. If the prediction is wrong, then the explanation must be changed.

ASKING ABOUT NATURE

Thousands of years ago, people looked up at the sky and wondered about what they were seeing. They wondered what the stars were. What caused day and night? Why did the sun rise and set each day? What caused the moon to change shape?

People also noticed other natural events. On Earth, there might be floods, earthquakes or volcanoes. What caused these events to happen?

Since ancient times, people have wondered about nature.

People also observed **patterns** in nature. Night always followed day. Spring always followed winter. Summer followed spring. Slowly, the weather would get cooler and days would grow shorter. Fall followed summer, and winter followed fall. Then this cycle would repeat again. A **cycle** is any pattern that keeps repeating itself.

APPLYING WHAT YOU HAVE LEARNED

★ What is a pattern? _____

_____

_____

★ Give one example of a pattern found in nature. _____

_____

_____

The seasons were not the only things in nature that had patterns and cycles. The weather had patterns, too. Clear skies sometimes filled with clouds. The sky would grow dark. Then it would rain. Thunder and lightning often came with the rain. Later, the rain would stop. Often a rainbow would appear in the sky after rain. Then the clouds would disappear. The sky would become clear again.

Often following a rain, a rainbow appears in the sky.

Living things also had patterns. In the fall, the leaves of many trees would turn yellow, orange, or red. Then they would drop off from the trees. In spring, the trees would grow buds. Some trees would have flowers. New leaves would appear on the trees. Soon, the tree tops would be thick again with new, fresh green leaves.

Animals also showed clear patterns. All animals seemed to need the same things to survive — food, water and shelter. They also seemed to go through different, but clearly recognizable stages, or **life cycles**. Some animals were hatched from eggs. Other animals came directly out of their mother's body.

Every animal began its life as a baby. The baby then grew larger and stronger. Some animals, like butterflies, actually changed their shape completely to become adults. Adult animals next had offspring of their own. The adults then grew older and weaker. Eventually, they would die.

An adult butterfly just after it comes out of its cocoon.

Ancient peoples observed these different patterns in nature. They developed their own stories to explain these patterns. They also made **predictions** about what would happen next based on these patterns.

APPLYING WHAT YOU HAVE LEARNED

★ Ancient Greeks thought the winter came when the daughter of the Earth Goddess went to the underworld for six months. How do you think this story helped them to explain what happened in winter?

_____

_____

_____

★ Create your own "ancient legend" to explain why day changes into night.

_____

_____

_____

★ Give two examples of repeating patterns in nature:

A. _____   B. _____

★ How do constantly repeating patterns in nature help us make predictions?

_____

_____

_____

THE BIRTH OF SCIENCE

Science began when people developed new ways to explain natural patterns and events. Science is based on the accurate **observation** of nature. When we observe, we learn through our senses (*sight, hearing, taste, touch, and smell*). Scientists then attempt to provide a **logical explanation** — an explanation that makes sense — to account for these observations. Scientists try to explain why things happen in nature. Scientific explanations must be supported by evidence. If a scientist observes something that does not fit with this explanation, then the explanation must be changed to account for the new observation.

Sometimes scientists use an explanation to make predictions. **A prediction** is a statement about what is going to happen in the future. If the prediction is correct, this gives further evidence in support of the scientific explanation. But if the prediction is incorrect, then the scientist has to change the explanation.

For example, some ancient peoples thought that night follows day because a giant serpent ate the sun. Each morning, the serpent spit the sun out. Scientists came up with a more logical explanation. As Earth moves in space, it turns on its axis. When an area of Earth faces the sun, it has day. When it turns away from the sun, that area has night. This explanation is logical and is based on actual observations.

APPLYING WHAT YOU HAVE LEARNED

★ Indicate on the blank line whether the statement is an observation, explanation or prediction:

• Yesterday, the sun rose at 6:00 A.M. _____

• Tomorrow, the sun will not rise at 6:00 A.M. _____

• The sun appears to rise because Earth spins on its axis. _____

★ Why do scientists have to change their explanations when they cannot explain an observation, or when their predictions fail?

_____

_____

WHAT YOU SHOULD KNOW

☐ You should know that there are different patterns in nature.

☐ You should know that patterns of repeating events in nature make predictions possible.

☐ You should know that science attempts to provide logical explanations of what happens in nature.

☐ You should know that scientific explanations are based on evidence. When an explanation is unable to explain an observation, the explanation must be changed.

☐ You should know that a scientific explanation can often be used to make a prediction. If the prediction is wrong, then the explanation must be changed.

LESSON STUDY CARDS

Below are two *Study Cards*. *Study Cards* are found at the end of each lesson. They highlight the most important information in that lesson. You should make a habit of copying these cards. On the back of the card, create your own diagram or picture. Also, make your own additional cards. These cards will help you to remember the most important concepts, facts, and relationships.

Observation of Nature

★ **Observations.** Anything that scientists see, hear, smell, touch, or taste in nature. Scientists record their observations to share with others.

★ **Patterns.** Certain events in nature repeat themselves in a particular order, like day following night.

★ **Predictions.** Based on patterns in nature, scientists can often predict what comes next.

What Is Science?

★ **Science.** Science is an attempt to explain the natural world. Scientific explanations are logical and are based on observations and other evidence.

★ **Logical Explanations.** An explanation is logical if it is reasonable.

★ **Changing Scientific Explanations.** If a scientific explanation cannot explain an observation or makes a wrong prediction, it must be changed.

CHECKING YOUR UNDERSTANDING

Day	Daily High Temperatures
Monday	22°C / 72°F
Tuesday	23°C / 74°F
Wednesday	24°C / 76°F
Thursday	?

1. Which is the best prediction of Thursday's high temperature?

   A   –2°C / 28°F   B   25°C / 77°F
   C   14°C / 58°F   D   50°C / 106°F

   S4.A
   2.1.3

 HINT *This question examines your ability to make predictions based on patterns in nature. Each day of the week, the temperature has increased by 1°C / 1.8°F. Based on this pattern, the temperature should increase from 24°C on Wednesday to 25°C on Thursday. Choice A, –2°C, is much too low if the temperature was 24°C on Wednesday. Choice C is also too low. Choice D, 50°C is much too high since the temperature was only 24°C on Wednesday. Therefore, the best answer is* **Choice B**.

Now answer some questions on your own. Circle the correct answer.

★ Ancient Greeks believed that the planets moved around Earth, but could not explain why they sometimes seemed to move backwards.

★ Later scientists concluded that Earth and other planets move around the sun, explaining why they sometimes seem to move backwards.

2. What can be concluded from these statements?

   A   Scientific knowledge has not really improved since ancient times.
   B   Experiments are more important to science than observations.
   C   When observations cannot be explained, scientists must change their explanations.
   D   The work of earlier scientists seldom influence later scientists.

   S4.A
   2.1.4

Use the illustrations below to answer question 3.

| January 10 | January 14 | January 18 | **?** January 22 |

3. Scientists have recorded the appearance of the moon from January 10 to January 18. Which picture is the best prediction of how the moon will appear on January 22?

S4.A
3.3.2

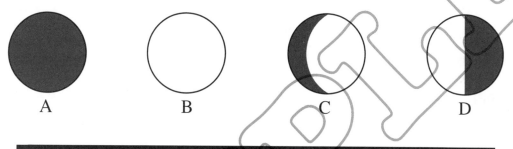

A   B   C   D

___

4. Which statement **best** describes a good scientific explanation?

   A   It does not need to be accurate.
   B   It must be supported by observations.
   C   It cannot be changed.
   D   It is not always logical.

   S4.A
   1.1.1

5. Scientific explanations are based in large part on observations. Which observation can be made about Earth, based on the photograph to the right?

   A   Earth is circular.
   B   Earth spins.
   C   Earth is made of rock.
   D   Earth has oxygen.

   S4.A
   3.3.1

6. What is a major goal of a scientist?

   A   to agree with other scientists even when they are inaccurate
   B   to earn a living working with chemicals
   C   to explain observable patterns in nature
   D   to create interesting stories

   S4.A
   3.3.1

7. Scientists often study patterns to make predictions. What season is missing from the Southern Hemisphere in the second picture?

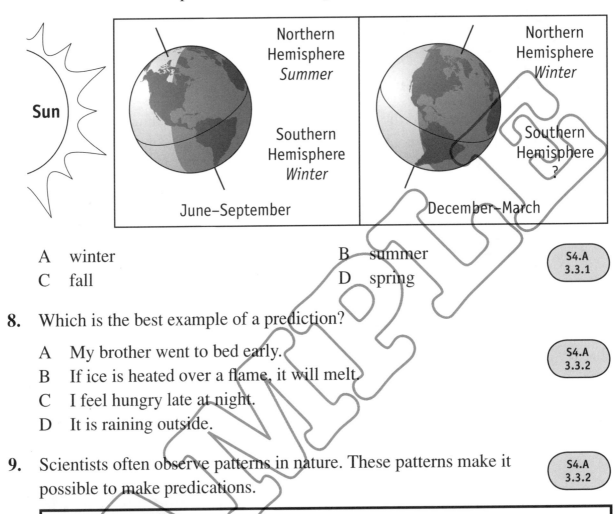

A   winter
C   fall

B   summer
D   spring

S4.A 3.3.1

8. Which is the best example of a prediction?

A   My brother went to bed early.

B   If ice is heated over a flame, it will melt.

C   I feel hungry late at night.

D   It is raining outside.

S4.A 3.3.2

9. Scientists often observe patterns in nature. These patterns make it possible to make predications.

S4.A 3.3.2

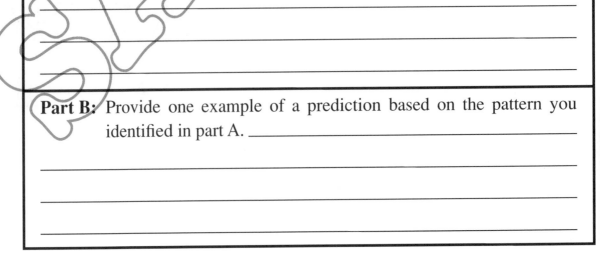

Part A: Identify one example of a pattern in nature. _____

_____

_____

Part B: Provide one example of a prediction based on the pattern you identified in part A. _____

_____

_____

SCIENTIFIC REASONING

In this lesson, you will learn more about how scientists think.

— IMPORTANT IDEAS —

A. **Scientific explanations** are based on facts. A **scientific fact** is supported by observations. A scientific fact can also be checked for accuracy. An **opinion** is an expression of feeling or belief that cannot be checked.

B. **Models** are diagrams, drawings or replicas that represent something else. They can be used to make observations, to test ideas, or to illustrate how a system works.

C. **Models** always differ in some ways from what they represent.

D. A **system** is a group of parts that work together to act as a whole. Systems can be **natural** or **human-made**.

FACT AND OPINION

In **Lesson 3**, you learned that scientific explanations are based on observable facts. Do you know what a fact is? Can you tell the difference between a fact and an opinion?

FACTS

A **fact** is a statement that can be checked to see if it is correct or true. *"Humans first landed on the moon on July 20, 1969."* This is a statement of fact. It can be checked.

A **scientific fact** is a statement that is supported by observation. Precise measurements often provide scientific facts. For example, a scientist may state that at the start of an experiment, water in a beaker was 22°C (72°F). This scientific fact is supported by an observation. The scientist used a thermometer to measure the temperature of the water. Other scientists could also have measured the temperature of this water, to check that it was 22°F. Scientists can then also repeat the same experiment, starting with a beaker of water at precisely 22°F.

A fact: Buzz Aldrin stepped on to the moon's surface, July 20, 1969.

A statement that clearly connects observations and results is also a fact. For example, a scientist at sea level might heat water until its temperature is 100°C (212°F). Then she sees that it boils. It is a **scientific fact** that the water boiled at this temperature. It is also a scientific fact that water will always boil at this temperature when heated at sea level.

OPINIONS

An **opinion** is a statement of personal feeling or belief. Words such as *think*, *feel*, and *believe* often indicate that a statement is an opinion. For example, this statement is an opinion: *"This water feels hot."* Different people have different views about what is hot. No one knows exactly what "hot" means. There is simply no way to check this. This type of opinion tells us the speaker's personal feeling or belief.

Writers sometimes make statements that look like facts but which are really opinions. Statements with phrases like "the best," or "the most interesting" express opinions, not facts. For example, "Our soap cleans the best." This statement looks like a fact, but it is really just an opinion.

There is a second kind of opinion. People give opinions about things they are currently unsure about. For example, "It will rain tonight" is an opinion. This second type of opinion may be supported by some facts. For example, the speaker may see dark, gray clouds in the sky. Later events or discoveries may prove or disprove this kind of opinion.

APPLYING WHAT YOU HAVE LEARNED

Below are several statements from a report by a scientist. Check the boxes below to show which statements are scientific facts (*supported by observations*) and which are expressions of opinion.

		Fact	Opinion
1.	Earth has one natural satellite, the moon.	☐	☐
2.	Earth rotates around its axis every 24 hours.	☐	☐
3.	The moon is quite beautiful.	☐	☐
4.	There is no wind on the moon.	☐	☐
5.	Astronomy is an interesting field of science.	☐	☐
6.	Someday, humans will travel to distant planets.	☐	☐
7.	Most people enjoy learning about science.	☐	☐

★ Write a factual statement of your own: _____

_____

_____

_____

★ Write an opinion statement of your own: _____

_____

_____

_____

MODELS

Scientists often use models to better understand what happens in nature. A **model** is a replica or copy, built or made to represent something else. For example, look at the model of the sun, Earth and moon on the next page.

There are many different kinds of models:

★ **Diagrams.** Some models are simple diagrams. A **concept map** is a model that shows how different ideas are related.

★ **Drawings.** A drawing may also be a model. A drawing of the inside of a volcano may show how the volcano works. This drawing is a model because it represents something else.

★ **Dioramas.** A diorama is a three-dimensional model. Often a diorama has a painted background with models of animals, figures, or trees in front of it. Many natural history museums have dioramas showing different types of wildlife in their natural setting. We might see elephants drinking in the African grasslands, or birds in the tops of trees in the Amazon rain forest. These dioramas help us to imagine what it would be like to be in another place.

Diorama of mountain gorillas at the American Museum of Natural History in New York City.

★ **Globes.** Globes are round, spherical models. They usually represent Earth. A globe might also represent the moon, another planet, or the sun. A group of globes can be arranged to show the positions of the planets in our solar system.

★ **Maps.** Maps are flat models that represent areas. Often a map shows the physical features of a place, such as the location of its mountains, lakes, rivers and deserts. Maps can also be used for finding directions or determining distances.

APPLYING WHAT YOU HAVE LEARNED

Can you match each type of model with what it represents?

1. Globe _____   A. a flat, two-dimensional model representing the physical features and distances of an area

2. Concept Map _____   B. a three-dimensional model showing how climate, wildlife and landforms of a place interact

3. Drawing _____   C. a round, spherical model used to represent Earth

4. Diorama _____   D. a flat, two-dimensional model representing how something works

5. Map _____   E. a model used to show how ideas are related to each other

HOW MODELS ARE USED

Usually a model is simpler than what it represents. For example, a model car looks like a real car, but is much smaller. The model car has the same shape, outside parts, and colors as the real car. A good model also usually has several parts. The parts of the model work together, just like the parts of the object or process they represent. Models can be used in several ways:

TO SEE RELATIONSHIPS

Scientists often use models to see relationships. For example, a model might have a light bulb in the middle to represent the sun. Earth might be represented by a small globe several feet from the light bulb. The moon might be represented by a smaller globe that circles around Earth. Here, scientists can see how the movements of these bodies are related.

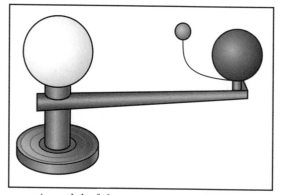

A model of the sun, moon, and Earth.

TO MAKE OBSERVATIONS

A model also can be used to make observations about how a system in nature works. In the example on the previous page, scientists can observe how the position of the moon affects the way it appears on Earth. By turning the light bulb (sun) on, scientists can use the model to understand and to explain why the moon seems to change its shape, and why there are *eclipses* — times when the moon appears to block out sunlight.

A **terrarium** is another example of a model that can be used to make observations. A terrarium is a closed glass container with plants, water, soil, and animals. For example, a terrarium might represent a pond. It has frogs, fish, and snails. It also has several plants usually found next to or in a pond. When the water evaporates, it forms droplets on the sides or inside the top of the terrarium. The water then falls back to the bottom. The plants create gases and food that the animals need. The animals create gases and nutrients that the plants

A small plant terrarium

need. Scientists can observe what happens in this terrarium in order to understand what happens in a real-life pond.

TO MAKE AND TEST PREDICTIONS

From a model, scientists can often make predictions about what will happen next. Then they can test their predictions with the model to see if they come true. The more closely a model resembles what it represents, the better its predictions will be.

The Three Gorges Dam. For example, scientists in China were about to build a very large dam on the Yangtze River to control flooding and to generate more hydroelectric power. They wanted to see what effects the dam would have before it was actually built. Building the actual dam was very expensive. So they built a large model of the dam.

A model of the Three Gorges Dam — the world's largest water conservation project.

The model had the same proportions as the actual dam, but it was much smaller in size. The scientists used the model of the dam to conduct several experiments before construction of the real dam began. They tried to predict its effects and test their predictions.

APPLYING WHAT YOU HAVE LEARNED

Think of an object or process you have learned about in science this year.

★ Describe how you would make a model to show it. _____

_____

_____

_____

★ Explain how your model makes this object or process easier to understand.

_____

_____

_____

_____

IMPROVING MODELS

Models are never exactly the same as the thing they represent. They always differ in some ways — such as in size, materials, or speed of movement. The *scale* of the model is how it relates to the object it represents in size.

For example, one inch of a model may represent one foot in length of the real object. Because models always differ from what they represent, models can always be improved. Therefore, when you examine a model, always ask yourself:

What is this model trying to show?	How closely does it show what it represents?	How might this model be improved?

To improve a model, it often helps to change the size or location of its parts. The parts should all be kept to the same scale. The model may also be improved by adding details. The more detailed a model is, the more closely it resembles what it represents.

APPLYING WHAT YOU HAVE LEARNED

In a model of our solar system, a tennis ball is used to represent Earth.

★ What would you use to represent the sun? _____

★ What would you use to represent the planet Mercury? _____

★ Where would you place these objects? _____

_____

SYSTEMS

Models are especially useful because they often help scientists understand systems. A **system** is any group of things that work together.

SYSTEMS IN NATURE

Many systems are found in nature:

★ **Human Digestive System.** Different parts of the human body, for example, work together to make up the digestive system. The mouth, teeth, esophagus, stomach and intestines work together to help the body digest food.

★ **Ecosystems.** All the plants, animals, land forms and weather in an area influence each other and work together. They form an **ecological system**, or **ecosystem**.

★ **Plants.** The different parts of a plant — its roots, stem, leaves, and seeds — work together as a single system to help the plant live, grow and reproduce.

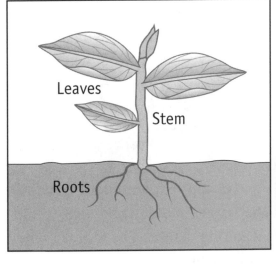

Leaves

Stem

Roots

★ **Solar System.** The sun and planets affect each other's movements in space and many of their characteristics. They make up the solar system.

APPLYING WHAT YOU HAVE LEARNED

★ Provide another example of a system found in nature. _____

_____

★ Why should this example be considered a system? _____

_____

_____

HUMAN-MADE SYSTEMS

Other systems are human-made:

★ **Ballpoint Pen.** A ballpoint pen has a metal tube filled with ink. The tube is
enclosed in a plastic holder or case. At the bottom or point of the tube is a tiny round ball, holding in the ink. When the ball rolls on paper, the ink flows out. The tube, ink, and ball point all work together to help us write.

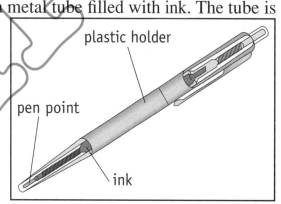

plastic holder

pen point

ink

★ **Simple Electrical Circuit.** Another example of a human-made system with several parts is a simple electric circuit. A battery provides electrical energy. This electricity travels through the wires. When it travels through the light bulb, the electricity makes the bulb light up. All these parts — the battery, wires, and bulb — work together as a system.

★ **Car.** A car is another human-made system with many parts that work together to make it run. Like the human body, a car actually has several systems — a braking system, an electrical system, a fuel system, an ignition system, an engine, and wheels. All of these work together.

APPLYING WHAT YOU HAVE LEARNED

★ Provide another example of a human-made system. _____

_____

★ Why should this example be considered a system? _____

_____

_____

In each of these natural and human-made systems, all of the parts work together towards the outcome. For example, all the parts of the digestive system help us to break up and digest the food we eat. If one part of a system changes, the system as a whole will also usually change. It may not even work.

APPLYING WHAT YOU HAVE LEARNED

★ In the electrical circuit shown on the previous page, describe what will happen to the light bulb if one of the wires is cut.

_____

_____

★ How does this show that the electrical circuit is a system? _____

_____

★ What could happen to a person's digestive system if one of its parts stops working? _____

_____

★ Why are all the parts of a system generally important to its overall operation? _____

_____

_____

WHY SCIENTIFIC KNOWLEDGE CHANGES

No claims or conclusions can be accepted by scientists unless they are supported by evidence. To decide how good a scientific explanation is, scientists look at the evidence from observations and experiments. As scientists collect more observations and data, their ideas and conclusions often change. For this reason, our scientific knowledge is constantly changing and improving.

WHAT YOU SHOULD KNOW

- [ ] You should know that scientific explanations are based on facts. A scientific fact is supported by observations and can be checked for accuracy. An opinion is an expression of feeling or belief that cannot be checked.

- [ ] You should know that models are diagrams, drawings or replicas that represent something else. They can be used to make observations, to test predictions, or to illustrate how a system works.

- [ ] You should know that models always differ in some ways from what they represent.

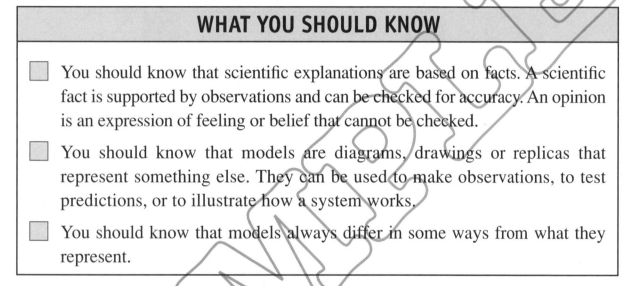

LESSON STUDY CARDS

Fact and Opinion

★ **Scientific Fact.** A scientific fact is a statement supported by observations.
  - It can be checked for accuracy.
  - A fact can be proven to be true or false.
  - For example: *It's 70°F outside today.*
★ **Opinion.** An opinion is an expression of belief or feeling.
  - It cannot be proven to be true or false.
  - For example: *I like eating pancakes.*

Models

★ Scientists use a model to represent something else — a process or object.
★ Models have different purposes. They can help scientists see relationships, make observations, or make and test their predictions about what will occur.
★ Models are usually made to scale. To improve a model you can often:
  - change the size and location of its parts.
  - make it more detailed, so that it more closely resembles what it represents.

CHECKING YOUR UNDERSTANDING

Four community groups in Pennsylvania recorded the number of owls seen in each of their cities in 2007. The graph below shows what they recorded:

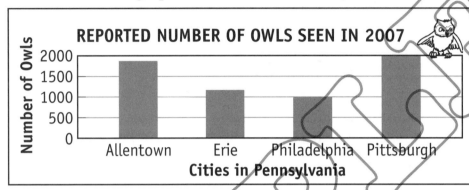

1. Which statement is a fact supported by information in the graph?

A   Allentown had the most beautiful owls.

B   Fewer owls were seen in Erie than in Philadelphia.

C   Owls were better fed in Pittsburgh than in Allentown

D   More than 1,500 owls were seen in Pittsburgh.

S4.A
1.1.1

HINT *This question tests your understanding of the difference between statements of fact and opinions. Choice A is an opinion, not a fact. It cannot be proven to be true. Choice B is a factual statement, but it is not supported by the information in the graph. According to the graph, more owls were seen in Erie than in Philadelphia. Choice C is also an opinion. It cannot be proven to be true. Choice D is a statement of fact that is also supported by the data. According to the graph, more than 1,500 owls were seen in Pittsburgh in 2007. Therefore, **Choice D** is the correct answer.*

Now answer some questions on your own. Circle the correct answer.

2. Which statement expresses an opinion?

A   Marie Curie discovered radium.

B   This book is 8 inches wide.

C   Our universe may not last forever.

D   The experiment ended at 12:35 P.M.

S4.A
1.1.1

Use the model below to answer questions 3 and 4.

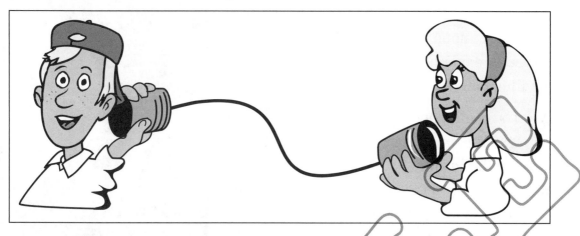

3. What does this model **best** represent?

    A   the human digestive system
    B   how fast light travels
    C   a model of the human ear
    D   a communications system

    ♦ Examine the Question
    ♦ Recall What You Know
    ♦ Apply What You Know

    S4.A
    3.2.1

4. Which observation can **most likely** be made from this model?

    A   Sound can travel through a string.
    B   The second student is a good listener.
    C   Sound travels better through water than through solid objects.
    D   Sound cannot travel in empty space.

    S4.A
    3.2.2

5. Many different systems, such as the digestive, nervous, and circulatory systems, work side by side in the human body. Which would be the best type of model for showing how the systems of the human body work together?

    A   a terrarium   B   a diorama
    C   a globe   D   a concept map

    S4.A
    3.2.3

6. How does a model differ from a system?

    A   A model is based on observation, while a system is based on facts.
    B   A model is based on nature, while a system is human-made.
    C   A model helps scientists understand something, while a system is any group of things working together.
    D   A model always has parts, while a system has no parts.

    S4.A
    3.2.3

7. A student is looking through a book on astronomy and sees a photograph taken in space of Earth, the moon and stars. Which statement correctly explains the sizes of the objects in the illustration?

A   The Earth appears smaller than the moon because it is smaller in size.

           S4.A 1.3.2

B   The stars appear larger than the moon because they are higher in the sky.

C   Earth appears to be the same size as the moon because Earth is closer in space.

D   The stars appear smaller than the moon because they are farther out in space.

Use the diagram below to answer question 8.

8. Which is a correct observation about the rainfall in the drawing?

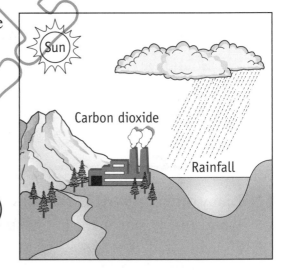

A   The sun causes rain to fall.

B   Rainfall falls from the clouds.

C   Factories provide most of the rainfall.

D   Carbon dioxide increases rainfall.

           S4.A 3.2.2

9. Which is the best example of a human-made system?

A   a piece of coal

B   a computer printer

C   a flowering plant

D   the digestive system

◆ **Examine the Question**
◆ **Recall What You Know**
◆ **Apply What You Know**

     S4.A 3.1.1

A teacher takes a class on a field trip to a nearby pond. To show the class how the human ear hears sounds, the teacher drops a stone into the pond. The stone hitting the water creates small waves in the pond. When the waves hit a leaf floating at the edge of the pond, the leaf begins to move back and forth.

10. In this model, what does the leaf represent?

A   a sound wave

B   the human brain

C   compressed air

D   a part of the ear

♦ **Examine the Question**
♦ **Recall What You Know**
♦ **Apply What You Know**

S4.A
3.2.1

11. Scientists use models for a number of different purposes.

S4.A
3.2.1

Part A: What is a model? _____

_____

_____

Part B: Identify one way in which scientists use models. _____

_____

_____

12. Scientists often use models to represent systems.

S4.A
3.2.3

Part A: Identify one example of a system. _____

_____

_____

Part B: Describe a model that might be used by scientists to explain how the system identified in part A works.

_____

_____

NATURE OF SCIENCE CONCEPT MAP

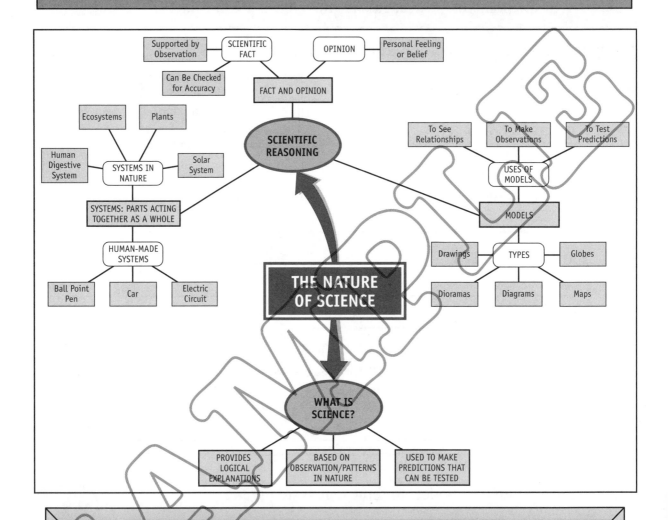

TESTING YOUR UNDERSTANDING

1. A student wants to conduct a scientific investigation about corn. Which question is precise enough for a scientific investigation?

    A   What is a corn plant?

    B   Does adding more water to corn plants make them grow faster?

    C   What type of corn plant has the best taste?

    D   Who invented popcorn?

S4.A
2.1.1

2. A student must think of a question for a science fair project. The question should be one that can be answered by conducting an experiment. Which question can **best** be answered by an experiment?

A   Where are volcanoes found?

B   How can you make a model airplane?

C   What is the fastest insect on Earth?

D   Does the weight of a paper airplane affect how far it can fly?

S4.A
2.1.1

3. Which is an example of a natural system?

A   the plants and animals in a pond

B   a typewriter and a piece of paper

C   a piece of string

D   a battery, wires, and a light bulb

S4.A
3.1.1

4. A scientist is studying birds. She concludes that two different types of birds living in a tree do not compete with each other for food. She records her observations in a chart:

Bird Type	Food	When They Feed	Where They Feed
1	insects	dawn, dusk	At the top of the tree
2	insects	dawn, dusk	At the bottom of the tree

What evidence **best** supports the scientist's conclusion?

A   There are enough insects for both types of birds.

B   These birds feed at different times.

C   These birds lay eggs at different times.

D   These birds feed in different parts of trees.

S4.A
2.1.4

5. Why should a bicycle be considered a system?

A   It has wheels.

B   It has parts that work together.

C   It is used to move people.

D   It can break down easily.

S4.A
3.1.1

Use the illustration below to answer question 6

6. A scientist examines the picture of a forest area after a fire. Which statement correctly predicts an effect that the damage to this forest will have?

    A   There will be a loss of sunshine.
    B   There will be a loss of wildlife.
    C   There will be flooding.
    D   There will be another fire.

    S4.A
    3.3.2

7. Which **best** describes a good scientific explanation?

    A   It is supported by evidence from observations.
    B   It does not always make sense.
    C   It cannot be changed in any way.
    D   It should not be repeated.

    S4.A
    1.1.1

Use the table below to answer question 8.

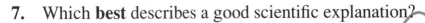

	Week 2	Week 3	Week 4	Week 5
Height of Plant A	5 inches	10 inches	15 inches	?
Height of Plant B	8 inches	12 inches	16 inches	?

8. Students recorded the heights of two plants at the end of each week. Which is the **best** prediction of the plants' heights at the end of week 5?

    A   Plant A will be taller than Plant B.
    B   Plant B will be taller than Plant A.
    C   Plants A and B will be the same height.
    D   Plants A and B will both decrease in height.

    S4.A
    3.3.2

9. Which statement is a scientific fact?

    A   Chocolate tastes better than popcorn.
    B   Elena's brother eats his lunch too quickly.
    C   There are many different kinds of plants.
    D   Studying science is very exciting.

    S4.A
    1.1.1

Use the diagram below to answer question 10.

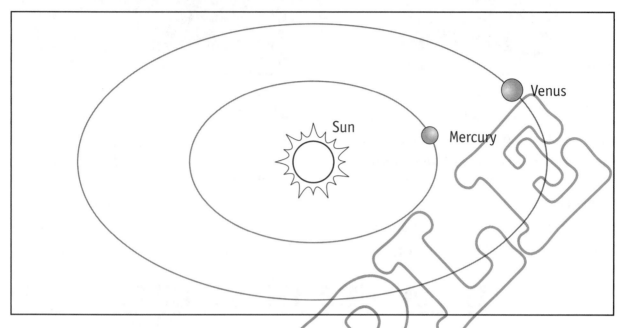

10. What does this diagram represent?

   A   the position of stars in the sky

   B   a section of the solar system

   C   how days on Earth occur

   D   the sun's position in our galaxy

   S4.A
   3.2.1

11. A model is generally simpler than the object or process it represents.

   S4.A
   3.2.1

   Part A: Give one example of a model representing an object or process.

   _____

   _____

   Part B: Describe one way in which the model you identified in part A
   might be improved.

   _____

   _____

   _____

   _____

CHECKLIST OF ELIGIBLE CONTENT

*At the end of each unit you will find a **Checklist of Eligible Content** like the one below. The purpose of these checklists are to help you monitor your understanding of major concepts and facts before going on to the next unit.*

Directions. Now that you have completed this unit, place a check (✔) next to those assessment anchors that you understand. If you are having trouble recalling information about any of these anchors, review the lesson shown in bold in the brackets.

THE NATURE OF SCIENCE

☐ **S4.A.1.1.1** Distinguish between a scientific fact and an opinion, providing clear explanations that connect observations and results (e.g., a scientific fact can be supported by making observations). **[Lesson 4]**

☐ **S4.A.2.1.4** State a conclusion that is consistent with the information/data. **[Lesson 3]**

☐ **S4.A.3.1.1** Categorize systems as either natural or human-made (e.g., ballpoint pens, simple electrical circuits, plant anatomy, water cycle). **[Lesson 4]**

☐ **S4.A.3.2.1** Identify what different models represent (e.g., maps show physical features, directions, distances; globes represent Earth; drawings of watersheds depict terrains; dioramas show ecosystems; concept maps show relationships of ideas). **[Lesson 3]**

☐ **S4.A.3.2.2** Use models to make observations to explain how systems work (e.g., water cycle, Sun-Earth-Moon system). **[Lesson 3]**

☐ **S4.A.3.3.1** Identify and describe observable patterns (e.g., growth patterns in plants, weather, water cycle. **[Lesson 3]**

☐ **S4.A.3.2.3** Use appropriate, simple modeling tools and techniques to describe or illustrate a system (e.g., two cans and string to model a communications system, terrarium to model an ecosystem. **[Lesson 3]**

☐ **S4.A.3.3.2** Predict future conditions/events based on observable patterns (e.g., day/night, seasons, sunrise/sunset, lunar phases. **[Lesson 3]**

UNIT 2

SCIENTIFIC INVESTIGATION AND TECHNOLOGY

In this unit, you will look at the processes of scientific investigation and technology. You will learn how scientists investigate nature and how engineers and technical designers create new products and solutions to meet our needs.

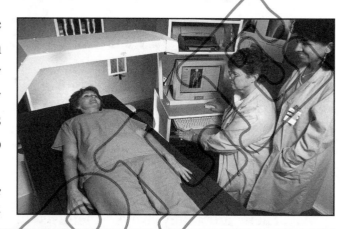

Science and technology are closely related to each other.

★ **Lesson 5: Designing a Scientific Investigation.** In this lesson, you will learn how scientists design an investigation by asking scientific questions and planning experiments and field investigations to answer them.

★ **Lesson 6: Conducting a Scientific Investigation.** In this lesson, you will learn how scientists conduct experiments and field investigations by making observations and taking precise measurements.

★ **Lesson 7: Analyzing the Results of a Scientific Investigation.** In this lesson, you will learn how scientists analyze their data, draw conclusions, and communicate their results to others.

★ **Lesson 8: Science and Technology.** In this lesson, you will learn how science and technology are related. You will also learn about the positive and negative impacts of technology on people and the environment.

KEY TERMS YOU WILL LEARN ABOUT IN THIS UNIT

- Observation
- Experiment
- Variable
- Microscope
- Hand Lens

- Binoculars
- Telescope
- Beaker
- Balance
- Mass

- Volume
- Hypothesis
- Technology
- Biotechnology
- Impact of Technology

LESSON 5

DESIGNING A SCIENTIFIC INVESTIGATION

In the next three lessons, you will learn about the process of scientific inquiry. In this lesson, you will learn how scientists ask scientific questions and design investigations. **Lessons 6** and **7** focus on how scientists take measurements and draw conclusions.

— IMPORTANT IDEAS —

A. There are many ways scientists investigate the natural world. These include observation, field investigations, and controlled experiments.

B. The following steps are often used by scientists to conduct an investigation:

★ A scientist observes the world and asks a **question**.

★ The scientist develops a **hypothesis** to answer the question.

★ The scientist designs an experiment or field investigation to test the hypothesis. Usually the investigation tests one **variable** at a time.

★ The scientist uses appropriate **tools** and **instruments** to carry out the investigation.

★ After the investigation, the scientist **organizes** and **interprets** the results, and draws **conclusions**.

★ The scientist **communicates** these results and conclusions to others.

TYPES OF SCIENTIFIC INVESTIGATIONS

There are many ways that scientists investigate nature.

OBSERVATION

One way scientists investigate nature is by **observing** it. For example, a scientist may look at the different types of clouds in the sky and record their shapes and other weather conditions. After several days, the scientist notices that when certain clouds appear, it often rains.

A scientist may also observe nature by using special tools. For example, with a **microscope**, a scientist can observe very tiny objects, like mineral crystals or living cells.

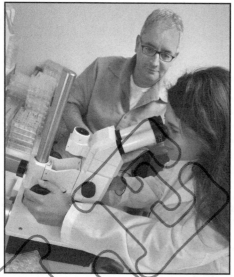

Scientists use powerful microscopes to observe very small objects.

DATA COLLECTION

Sometimes scientists just observe and describe what they see, hear, smell, or touch. At other times, they use special tools to **measure** what they observe. For example, they may use a **ruler** to measure an object's length. They measure *change* by recording how much something changes in size, position, or temperature. The precise measurements that scientists collect and record over time are referred to as **data**.

FIELD INVESTIGATIONS vs. CONTROLLED EXPERIMENTS

A scientist may go out into the natural world to collect data. This process is known as a **field investigation**. For example, a scientist may go to the desert to discover what plants grow there. At other times, a scientist may design special tests that are conducted in a closed laboratory, where conditions can be controlled. For example, a scientist may combine different chemicals, or observe the effects of light on the growth of plants. This kind of investigation is known as a **controlled experiment**.

RECORD-KEEPING

When scientists make observations and collect data, they **record** their results. They need to record these results to provide evidence to support their conclusions. Often, scientists keep their information in a **log** or **notebook**. These records must accurately state what the scientists have done and the results they received. This allows other scientists to review what has been done. These other scientists can then repeat the experiment or conduct a similar investigation to see if they reach the same results.

APPLYING WHAT YOU HAVE LEARNED

Define the following terms. This will help you to create your own scientific glossary. Add new terms of your own as you read this book:

GLOSSARY ON SCIENTIFIC INVESTIGATION

Scientific Term	Definition of the Term
Observation:	
Data Collection:	
Field Investigation:	
Controlled Experiment:	
Record-keeping:	

CHOOSING THE BEST APPROACH

The type of investigation that a scientist conducts often depends on the question that the scientist is trying to answer.

OBSERVATION OF NATURE

To answer some questions, scientists simply go into the natural world to observe events and collect data. This approach is best for exploring what happens in nature. For example, if scientists are trying to understand how tadpoles turn into frogs, they can observe tadpoles in a pond.

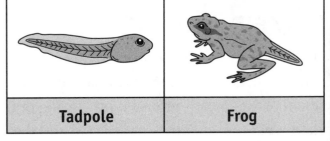

| Tadpole | Frog |

CONTROLLED EXPERIMENT

In a **controlled experiment**, scientists actively change something to see the effect this change has. This approach works best for seeing how two or more things are related. For example, suppose scientists want to see what effect a chemical has on plant growth. First, they get several plants of the same type. These plants are placed in pots with identical soil in the laboratory. Each plant receives the same amount of water and sunlight.

★ Some of the plants are placed in soil *without* the chemical. They form the "control group."

★ Other plants are placed in soil *with* the chemical. These plants form the "experimental group."

The scientists then observe and compare what happens to each group of plants. The scientists also measure the size of each plant at fixed periods, to see what effect the chemical is having on plant growth. You will learn more about how to conduct an experiment later in this lesson.

APPLYING WHAT YOU HAVE LEARNED

★ Look at the list of questions that follows. Each question is one that scientists wish to answer.

• Determine whether scientists should *observe nature* or conduct a *controlled experiment* as the best way to answer the question.

• Then explain why you chose that approach.

1. How long does it take Jupiter to circle the sun?

☐ Observation of nature   ☐ Controlled experiment

Explain your answer: _____

_____

APPLYING WHAT YOU HAVE LEARNED

2. Which fertilizer best promotes the growth of bean plants?

☐ Observation of nature ☐ Controlled experiment

Explain your answer: _____

_____

_____

3. What types of rocks are found in the Appalachian Mountains?

☐ Observation of nature ☐ Controlled experiment

Explain your answer: _____

_____

_____

★ What conclusions can you reach about which questions are best answered by the observation of nature (*or field investigations*) and which ones are best answered by a controlled experiment?

_____

_____

_____

_____

STEPS OF A SCIENTIFIC INVESTIGATION

Scientific inquiry usually begins with observation of the natural world. Scientists then ask themselves questions about what they observe. Scientists next try to answer their questions by building models, making observations, collecting data, or conducting experiments. For example, a scientist might watch children fly paper airplanes and ask:

How can a paper airplane be made to fly a longer distance?

Suppose that the scientist decides to answer this question by conducting a controlled experiment. There is no single, fixed method for all experiments. However, many scientists use the steps below to conduct an experiment or field investigation.

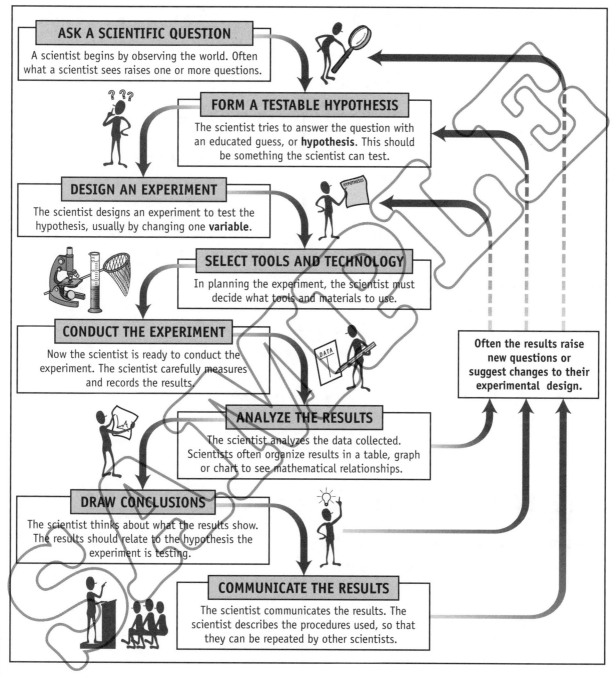

ASK A SCIENTIFIC QUESTION
A scientist begins by observing the world. Often what a scientist sees raises one or more questions.

FORM A TESTABLE HYPOTHESIS
The scientist tries to answer the question with an educated guess, or **hypothesis**. This should be something the scientist can test.

DESIGN AN EXPERIMENT
The scientist designs an experiment to test the hypothesis, usually by changing one **variable**.

SELECT TOOLS AND TECHNOLOGY
In planning the experiment, the scientist must decide what tools and materials to use.

CONDUCT THE EXPERIMENT
Now the scientist is ready to conduct the experiment. The scientist carefully measures and records the results.

ANALYZE THE RESULTS
The scientist analyzes the data collected. Scientists often organize results in a table, graph or chart to see mathematical relationships.

DRAW CONCLUSIONS
The scientist thinks about what the results show. The results should relate to the hypothesis the experiment is testing.

COMMUNICATE THE RESULTS
The scientist communicates the results. The scientist describes the procedures used, so that they can be repeated by other scientists.

Often the results raise new questions or suggest changes to their experimental design.

Let's look more closely at each of these steps. The rest of this lesson will focus on designing an experiment — the first four steps above. **Lessons 6** and **7** will focus on collecting and analyzing the data and drawing conclusions — the last four steps.

Suppose you are interested in flying paper airplanes. How can you create an experiment for studying the design of a paper airplane?

ASK A WELL-DEFINED QUESTION

Only well-defined questions can be tested by an experiment. Vague questions cannot be answered by a scientific investigation. Questions for an experiment must be *specific* and *factual*. They must identify *exactly* what will determined by the investigation.

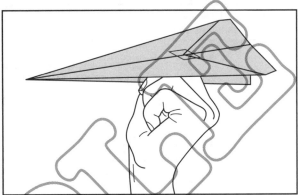

For example, the following question is **not** precise enough for a specific experiment: *What is the best paper airplane?* A scientist would wonder what "best" means. Does it mean the prettiest? Or does it mean the most expensive? Instead, a more well-defined question would be:

> *Will a paper airplane fly a longer distance*
> *if it has a flat nose or a pointed nose?*

This question is very precise. The scientist is asked to compare the effects of two specific types of "noses" on how far a paper airplane flies.

MAKE A TESTABLE HYPOTHESIS

A **hypothesis** is an educated guess that attempts to answer the question. A good hypothesis can be **tested** by an experiment. For example, a scientist may make the hypothesis that *a paper airplane will fly farther with a pointy nose than with a flat nose*. This hypothesis can be tested by an experiment. An experiment may

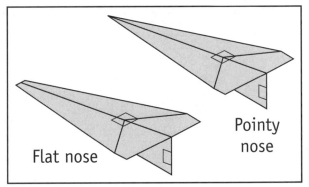

Flat nose

Pointy nose

show that the hypothesis is either right or wrong. In science, proving a hypothesis is wrong can be just as valuable as proving it is right.

APPLYING WHAT YOU HAVE LEARNED

★ Why can it be just as important to prove that a hypothesis is wrong as it is to prove that it is right? _____

_____

_____

★ Think of an experiment you did in science class this year. What hypothesis did that experiment test? _____

_____

_____

PLAN THE EXPERIMENT

An experiment creates special conditions to test the hypothesis. It is important to plan the experiment carefully.

VARIABLES

A **variable** is anything that can change in the experiment. In most experiments, a scientist changes one variable to see what effect this has on something else. The scientist then observes the effect of this change.

For example, a researcher conducting an experiment on paper airplanes could change these variables:

What kind of paper should the airplane be made of?

What is the shape of the paper airplane?

How do experiments build scientific knowledge?

In most experiments, a scientist changes only **one variable**. For example, in an experiment on paper airplanes, a scientist will pick one variable — such as whether the plane has a flat or pointy nose. The scientist will change *only* this variable and see how this affects something else — such as how far the airplane will fly. Because this distance may change, it becomes a **second variable** in this experiment.

All other conditions are kept exactly the same. Each plane should be the same size, be made of the same type of paper, and have the same shape except for the nose. Keeping all the other conditions the same allows the scientist to see the precise effects that the changes in **one variable** have on **another variable** (*the distance the airplane flies*).

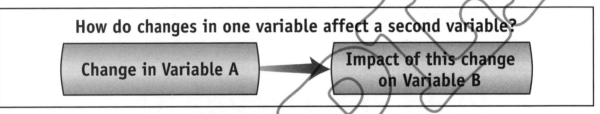

You can think of an experiment as a **comparison**. The scientist observes the changes in the variable being tested, and observes the results.

APPLYING WHAT YOU HAVE LEARNED

For each example below, identify the question the scientist is investigating:

Variable the scientist changes	Variable the scientist measures	What question is the scientist trying to answer?
Type of nose a paper airplane has	Distance the paper airplane can fly	
Amount of air in a sealed container	Amount of time a candle in the container will burn	
Type of soil	Amount of soil erosion in a heavy rainfall	

In many experiments, the scientist creates one group where the variable is not changed. This is called the "control" group. In a second group, the variable is changed. This second group is called the "experimental" group.

CHOOSE APPROPRIATE TOOLS AND INSTRUMENTS

Designing an investigation is like making a recipe. First you must identify the materials, tools, and instruments that are needed. Then you must list the steps to be followed to conduct the investigation or experiment.

ELEMENTS OF A GOOD EXPERIMENTAL DESIGN

★ The experiment tests the hypothesis.

★ All the variables are identified. Usually, only one variable is changed.

★ All required materials and instruments are listed.

★ Results can be precisely measured.

Will a paper airplane fly a longer distance
if it has a flat nose or a pointed nose?

A. To begin this experiment, you need: (1) two pieces of paper that are identical in size; (2) a roll of transparent tape; (3) a ruler. Start by making two paper airplanes with pointy noses that are exactly the same. Here is how it is done:

Step 1: **Step 2:** **Step 3:** **Step 4:**

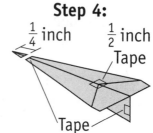

B. Then cut off the first ¼ inch piece from only one of your two planes, giving it a "flat" nose. Attach the piece of paper you cut off to the fold in the center of that plane, so that its weight stays the same. Tape the central fold together on both planes.

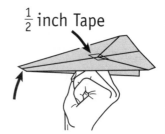

C. Now you are ready to test your airplanes. Toss each plane from an identical location using the same force.

D. Measure and record the distance each paper airplane travels after it lands. Repeat the experiment several times with each paper airplane.

Record your notes in the following table:

Type of Plane	Distance Flown Trial #1	Distance Flown Trial #2	Distance Flown Trial #3	Distance Flown Trial #4
"Pointy-Nosed" Plane				
"Flat-Nosed" Plane				

STANDARD LABORATORY AND FIELD INSTRUMENTS

In conducting experiments and field investigations, scientists often use special tools. The following are some of the standard scientific tools and instruments.

Magnifiers for Making Observations

★ **Microscope.** An instrument that uses a series of lenses to magnify specimens placed on slides.

★ **Hand Lens.** A magnifying glass used to inspect the features of something more closely.

★ **Binoculars.** An instrument that uses lenses to magnify distant objects, like wildlife.

★ **Telescope.** An instrument that uses lenses to magnify very distant objects, like stars or planets.

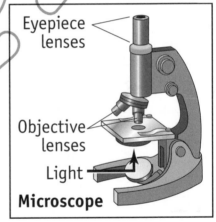

Microscope

Equipment for Safety

★ **Safety Goggles.** Plastic goggles large enough to protect the eyes and face during an experiment from fine dust, splashes, mists, or sprays.

★ **Laboratory Aprons.** Worn over clothing to protect clothing and the skin from splashes, spilled chemicals or biological materials.

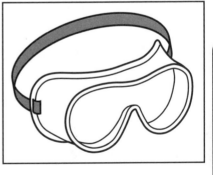

Equipment for Taking Measurements

★ **Ruler.** A stick marked in inches and feet, or in centimeters, used to measure length.

★ **Beaker.** A glass container that can be used to measure volume.

★ **Thermometer.** An instrument used to measure temperatures in degrees.

★ **Balance.** An instrument, usually with one or two pans, used to measure the mass of an object.

★ **Spring Scale.** A scale that measures the weight of an object by seeing how much it pulls on a steel spring attached to a dial.

★ **Timers.** Clocks, stop watches or other devices that precisely measure the passage of time in seconds, minutes, and hours.

APPLYING WHAT YOU HAVE LEARNED

Fill in the information called for in the chart on this and the following page:

Equipment	How It Looks	What Is It Used For?
1. Safety goggles		
2. Binoculars		
3. Hand lens		
4. Spring scale		
5. Balance		
6. Thermometer		

APPLYING WHAT YOU HAVE LEARNED

Equipment	How It Looks	What Is It Used For?
7. Stopwatch		
8. Telescope		
9. Beaker		
10. Ruler		

WHAT YOU SHOULD KNOW

A. You should know that scientists ask questions about the natural world and try to answer them through scientific investigation.

B. You should know that scientists often use certain steps to carry out a scientific investigation or experiment:

The scientist observes nature and asks a well-defined question.

From these observations, the scientist develops a hypothesis or educated guess to try to answer the question.

The scientist then designs an experiment or field investigation to test the hypothesis. A controlled experiment often changes one variable to see what effect this has on a second variable. All other experimental conditions are kept exactly the same.

Tools that scientists often use in their investigations include hand lenses, microscopes, binoculars, telescopes, safety goggles, rulers, balances, beakers, and thermometers.

LESSON STUDY CARDS

Steps in a Scientific Investigation

★ Ask a well-defined scientific question

★ Form a testable hypothesis

★ Design an experiment or field investigation to test the hypothesis by changing a variable

★ Select tools and materials

★ Conduct the experiment and collect data

★ Analyze data

★ Form conclusions

★ Communicate results

Designing Scientific Investigations

★ **Hypothesis.** An educated guess that tries to answer a question under investigation.

★ **Variable.** A variable is something that can be changed or varied to find how that change affects other things in the experiment.

★ **Scientific Tools and Equipment.** These tools include:

- balance
- thermometer
- binoculars
- scale
- ruler
- hand lens
- telescope
- beaker

CHECKING YOUR UNDERSTANDING

Juan gives one group of 10 chickens a type of chicken feed that has no protein. He gives a second group of 10 chickens the exact same amount of chicken feed each day, but he adds a small amount of protein powder. He weighs both groups of chickens at the start of the experiment. Two months later, he weighs both groups again.

1. What question is Juan trying to answer in this experiment?

   A   Will protein powder cause chickens to live longer?

   B   Does protein powder cause chickens to gain weight?

   C   Do chickens prefer chicken feed with protein powder?

   D   Can chickens become stronger by eating protein powder?

S4.A
2.1.1

HINT

This question looks at the methods used by scientists to carry out a scientific investigation. You should understand that an experiment usually looks at the effects that changing one thing or variable has on another variable. In this question, only one variable has been changed — some chickens have protein powder added to their feed. The scientist then weighs the chickens. The experiment tests whether chickens eating protein powder will gain more weight. Therefore, the best answer is B.

Now answer some questions on your own. Circle the correct answer.

2. A teacher creates a track of 50 meters. A student wants to measure the time it takes to run that distance. What instrument should the student use?

A   a ruler

B   a telescope

C   a thermometer

D   a stop watch

> ◆ Examine the Question
> ◆ Recall What You Know
> ◆ Apply What You Know

S4.A 2.2.1

Use the information below to answer questions 3 and 4.

3. A student in a science class places a wooden spoon and a stainless steel spoon in a container of boiling water. She waits five minutes and then measures the temperature at the end of the handle of each spoon. Which instrument should the student use to measure the temperature of the spoon handles?

A   a telescope

B   a thermometer

C   a ruler

D   a balance

S4.A 2.2.1

4. In the experiment described above, what question is the student trying to answer?

A   Can water conduct heat?

B   Does steel conduct heat better than wood?

C   Does wood conduct electricity better than steel?

D   Does heat cause either wood or steel to expand?

S4.A 2.1.1

5. James has decided to investigate whether the number of flowers on a plant will increase if more water is given to the plant. James has ten pots of geraniums to use in this experiment. What condition should be changed for some of the plants to investigate the question?

A   amount of water

B   temperature of the water

C   number of hours in sunlight

D   type of soil

S4.A 2.1.2

6. Alice places a magnet next to a metal fork. She records what happens. Next, she places the same magnet next to a fork made of plastic. She records what happens next. Which question is Alice **most likely** investigating with this experiment?

A   How do different materials react to magnets?

B   What causes magnets to be attracted to metal objects?

C   Does the size of the magnet affect its power?

D   Do some objects other than magnets have magnetic power?

S4.A 2.1.1

7. A student has to present a project for her school's science fair. She must ask a question that can be investigated by conducting an experiment. Which question can she **best** investigate with an experiment?

A   What are Pennsylvania's major land forms?

B   What type of pizza has the best taste?

C   How does rainwater become groundwater?

D   Does the amount of light a bean plant receives affect its growth?

S4.A 2.1.1

8. Which example would **NOT** be considered a scientific investigation?

A   Describing which kind of music sounds the most beautiful.

B   Sorting and labeling a collection of insects.

C   Testing different materials with a magnet to see which are magnetic.

D   Testing different foods to find out how much fat they contain.

S4.A 2.1.1

9. A scientist conducts an experiment to find out how much light carrot plants need to grow. Which should the scientist use as a variable?

A   the temperature the plants are kept at

B   the amount of sunlight the plants receive

C   the amount of water each plant is given

D   the kind of soil the plant is placed in

S4.A 2.1.2

10. Almost every experiment begins with a scientist setting out to find the answer to a particular question.

S4.A
2.1.1
2.1.2

> **Part A:** Identify a question that a scientist might investigate with an experiment.
>
> _____
>
> _____
>
> **Part B:** Describe one variable a scientist might change in the experiment you identified in part A.
>
> _____
>
> _____

11. Three balls of clay are shot out of a spoon launcher. Each ball of clay is a different size. The table below shows the distances the pieces of clay traveled.

S4.A
2.2.1
2.1.1

Distances Pieces of Clay Traveled

Size of Clay Ball	First Launch	Second Launch	Third Launch	Average Distance Traveled
Small	76 inches	80 inches	85 inches	80 inches
Medium	50 inches	42 inches	46 inches	46 inches
Large	8 inches	16 inches	12 inches	12 inches

> **Part A:** Identify one tool used to make measurements in this investigation.
>
> _____
>
> **Part B:** What question is this experiment investigating? _____
>
> _____
>
> _____
>
> _____

LESSON 6

CONDUCTING A SCIENTIFIC INVESTIGATION

In **Lesson 5**, you learned how scientists design experiments to test hypotheses and answer scientific questions. In this lesson, you will learn how scientists conduct experiments by making observations, taking measurements, and recording their findings.

— IMPORTANT IDEAS —

A. Scientists use their five senses to make **observations**.

B. Scientists often use special instruments to take measurements:

★ **Distance:** Scientists use rulers or meter sticks.

★ **Weight:** Scientists use spring scales.

★ **Volume:** Scientists use beakers.

★ **Temperature:** Scientists use thermometers.

C. Scientists generally use **metric units** of measurement.

D. Scientists observe and record **change** by recording the passage of time along with other measurements.

To conduct an experiment, scientists usually bring their materials and instruments together in a specific order. They record each step as they proceed so that other scientists can repeat the same investigation.

It is very important that scientists follow each step of their experimental design in turn. Results may be different if the steps of the experiment are conducted in a different order. Scientists must also be aware of safety at all times. For example, a scientist mixing chemicals in a laboratory should always wear safety goggles.

Usually, scientists conducting an investigation try to see how changes in one variable will affect a second variable. The scientists therefore must carefully record what changes they make to the first variable. Then they must carefully observe or measure what changes take place in the second variable.

In many investigations, scientists simply **observe** what happens. This means they use one or more of their five senses to tell what is happening.

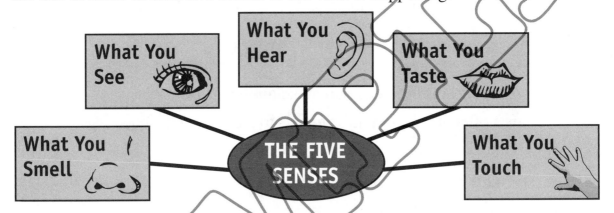

Scientists often use special tools to improve their observations. For example, scientists may look through a **telescope** to observe distant stars. They may use **binoculars** to observe animal behavior from a distance. Scientists may closely inspect a plant leaf with a **hand lens** in the laboratory.

Based on their observations, scientists may make predictions that can be tested by still further observations. For example, scientists might predict what types of plants some animals will eat, or where a planet will next appear in the sky.

APPLYING WHAT YOU HAVE LEARNED

Directions: Match the correct tool with what it is used for.

1. Hand lens _____
2. Microscope _____
3. Binoculars _____
4. Telescope _____

A. to observe a group of deer eating in a forest
B. to observe craters on the surface of the moon
C. to observe spores on a piece of moldy bread
D. to observe close-up the parts of a dragonfly

TAKING MEASUREMENTS

During an experiment or field investigation, scientists often take very precise measurements. This helps them to understand what is occurring. Scientists often measure:

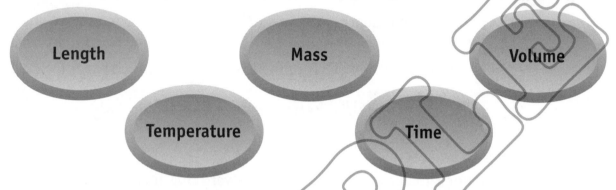

Length   **Mass**   **Volume**

Temperature   **Time**

UNITS OF MEASUREMENT

Taking precise measurements is an important part of most scientific investigations. Most Americans use the "English" system of measurement:

Length	Weight	Volume	Temperature
inch, foot, yard, mile	ounce, pound, ton	pint, cup, quart, gallon	degrees Fahrenheit (°F)

Scientists around the world generally prefer the **metric system** of measurement:

★ **Length**. A **meter** is just over 3 feet. One **inch** is equal to 2.54 centimeters.

   • 1,000 **millimeters** (mm) = 1 meter (m)
   • 100 **centimeters** (cm) = 1 meter (m)
   • 1 **kilometer** (km) = 1,000 meters (m)

★ **Mass**. A **kilogram** is about 2.2 pounds.

   • 1 **kilogram** (kg) = 1,000 grams (g)

You might have noticed that when *kilo* is used, it means one thousand.

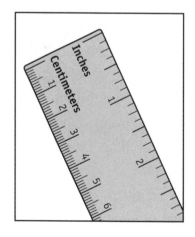

★ **Volume.** A **liter** is a little more than 1 quart.

  • 1,000 **milliliters** (mL) = 1 **liter** (L)

> You might have also noticed that when *milli* is used, it means one thousandth (1/1000): *milli*liter, *milli*meter.

★ **Temperature.** Scientists measure temperature in degrees **Celsius**.

  • 100°C = one hundred degrees Celsius (212°F, or the temperature at which water boils at sea level)

  • 0°C = zero degrees Celsius (32°F, or the temperature at which water freezes)

APPLYING WHAT YOU HAVE LEARNED

★ Which is longer?

  • 1 foot or 1 meter: _____   • 1 yard or 1 meter: _____

★ Which is heavier?

  • 6 pounds or 3 kilograms: _____   • 1 gram or 1 ounce: _____

★ Which is warmer?

  • 100°F or 100°C: _____   • 40°F or 0°C: _____

MEASURING LENGTH OR DISTANCE

To find the **length** of something, scientists use a ruler or meter stick. To measure length, find the first line (known as the 0 mark) to the left of the ruler. Then place your object starting at this mark. Look at where the object ends on your ruler. Write down the number just below that ending point. Then count the narrow, shorter lines between that number and the end of your object. If the number is

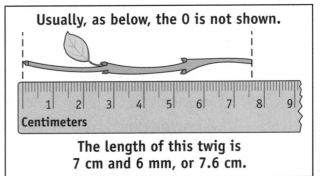

Usually, as below, the 0 is not shown.

The length of this twig is 7 cm and 6 mm, or 7.6 cm.

in centimeters, the lines represent millimeters. You can combine the centimeters and millimeters together by using a **decimal point**: *centimeters.millimeters*. This gives you the length in centimeters (cm).

APPLYING WHAT YOU HAVE LEARNED

★ What is the length of the worm?

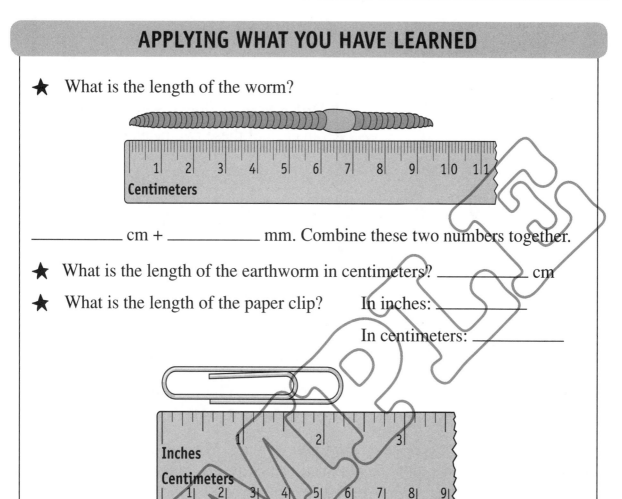

_____ cm + _____ mm. Combine these two numbers together.

★ What is the length of the earthworm in centimeters? _____ cm

★ What is the length of the paper clip?   In inches: _____

In centimeters: _____

MEASURING VOLUME

Volume is how much space something takes up. To measure the volume of a liquid, scientists pour the liquid into either a **beaker** or graduated cylinder. The beaker often has lines every 5 mL (*milliliters*). The surface of the liquid curves up the sides of the beaker. Measure the volume of the liquid from the bottom of the curve. See which line from the side of the beaker is closest to this level.

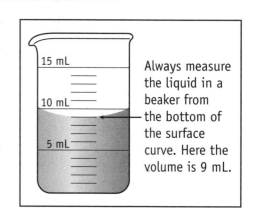

Always measure the liquid in a beaker from the bottom of the surface curve. Here the volume is 9 mL.

APPLYING WHAT YOU HAVE LEARNED

Beaker A	Beaker B
90	90
80	80
70	70
60	60
50	50
40	40
30	30
20	20
10	10

Beaker A   **Beaker B**

What is the volume of water contained in each of these two beakers?

A. _____ mL

B. _____ mL

WEIGHT AND MASS

Weight is how heavy an object is. Weight is created by the pull of gravity. It measures how strongly gravity pulls the object towards Earth's center.

An object's weight is related directly to its mass. **Mass** is the amount of matter the object has. An object with greater mass is heavier than an object with less mass.

APPLYING WHAT YOU HAVE LEARNED

Weight and mass seem very similar, but in fact they are different. For example, the moon is one-quarter the size of Earth. Thus, the moon's gravity is less than Earth's gravity. As a result, your weight on the moon is less than your weight on Earth. However, your mass remains the same. Why is this?

_____

_____

_____

_____

_____

MEASURING WEIGHT

Weight is measured by a **scale**. A scale measures the pull of gravity on an object.

Spring Scale. Scientists often use a **spring scale** to measure the weight of an object. The object is attached to the spring. The weight of the object pulls on the spring. As it pulls, an indicator points to a number. The number on the scale shows the weight of the object.

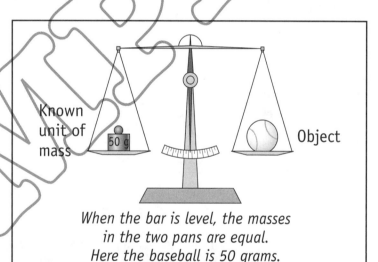

Spring Scale

MEASURING MASS

Scientists use a **balance** to measure mass. A **balance** puts a known mass on one side and the object to be measured on the other side.

Double-Pan Balance. A double-pan balance has a bar with pans on each side. The scientist puts the object to be measured in one pan. In the other pan, the scientist puts known units of mass. Units of mass are added until the bar is level — both pans are at the same height. The scientist then adds up all the known units to find the mass of the object.

Known unit of mass

50 g

Object

When the bar is level, the masses in the two pans are equal. Here the baseball is 50 grams.

APPLYING WHAT YOU HAVE LEARNED

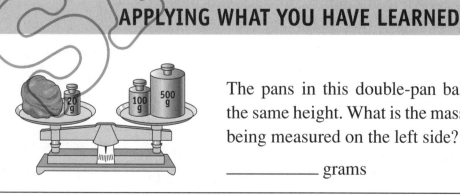

The pans in this double-pan balance are at the same height. What is the mass of the rock being measured on the left side?

_____ grams

A **Triple-Beam Balance.** A triple-beam balance has a single pan. Three beams with "riders" are used to measure the mass of whatever is placed in the pan. The riders are moved along notches on each beam.

How do you find the mass of the object in the pan? Simply add up the numbers shown on the three riders of the triple-beam balance.

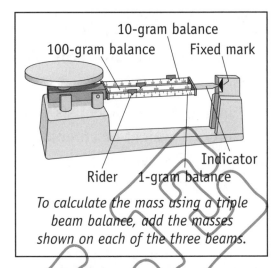

To calculate the mass using a triple beam balance, add the masses shown on each of the three beams.

APPLYING WHAT YOU HAVE LEARNED

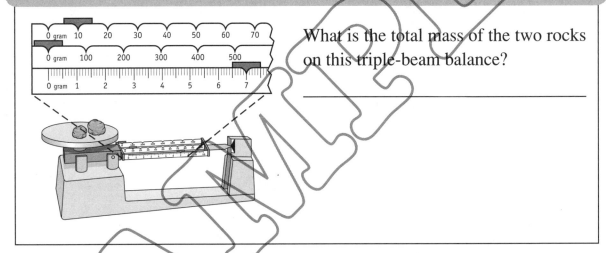

What is the total mass of the two rocks on this triple-beam balance?

_____

MEASURING TEMPERATURE

Temperature tells how hot or cold an object is. To measure temperature, scientists use a **thermometer**. There are many kinds of thermometers.

Many thermometers are glass tubes with colored liquid inside. Numbers are printed along the side of the tube. As the thermometer gets warmer, the liquid expands and rises. To measure the temperature, look at the top of the liquid column keeping your eye at the same level as the liquid. Then read the

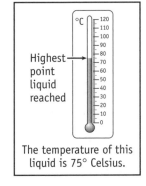

The temperature of this liquid is 75° Celsius.

number of degrees closest to the top of the liquid. Scientists usually use the **Celsius** scale. Water freezes at 0°C (32°F) and boils at 100°C (212°F).

APPLYING WHAT YOU HAVE LEARNED

★ What is the temperature shown in each of the following thermometers?

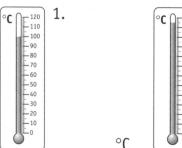

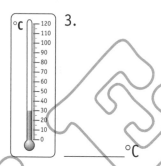

1. _____ °C

2. _____ °C

3. _____ °C

★ Which of these thermometers shows the boiling point of water?

_____

MEASURING TIME

Scientists may also record the time between their observations, measurements, or events. Time can be measured in seconds, minutes, days or even years. For example, how much does a plant grow *each week*? Or what distance does a planet travel in space in *one year*? Knowing the length of time helps scientists know how fast or slowly a change is occurring. You will learn more about measuring speed and motion later in this book.

APPLYING WHAT YOU HAVE LEARNED

★ Complete the following table by indicating the most appropriate tool for each type of measurement.

What is being measured	Most Appropriate Tool
To measure the lengths of a butterfly's wings	
To measure the mass of a common earthworm	
To measure the volume of a glass of milk	
To measure the temperature inside a refrigerator	

WHAT YOU SHOULD KNOW

☐ You should know that to make observations, scientists use their five senses. They may also use tools like microscopes, telescopes, binoculars, and hand lenses.

☐ You should know that to measure length, scientists often use a ruler, meter stick or centimeter ruler. To measure volume, they often use a beaker. To measure mass, they use a double-pan or triple-beam balance. To measure weight, scientists use a spring scale. To measure temperature, they use a thermometer.

LESSON STUDY CARDS

Measuring Data

★ **English System**
  • **Length:** inches, feet, yards, miles
  • **Volume:** cups, pints, quarts, gallons
  • **Weight:** pounds, tons
★ **Metric System**
  • **Length:** mm, cm, m, km.
  • **Volume:** liter (L), milliliter (mL)
  • **Mass:** grams (g) or kilograms (kg)
  • **Temperature:** degrees in Celsius (°C)

Scientific Instruments Used For Measurement

★ **Length:** ruler or a meter stick

★ **Volume:** a beaker

★ **Weight:** a spring scale

★ **Mass:** double pan or triple-beam balance

★ **Temperature:** a thermometer

CHECKING YOUR UNDERSTANDING

1. A teacher brings a pine cone from the forest into science class. The students want to measure the mass of the pine cone. Which statement correctly identifies the **best** tool to use to make this measurement?

    A   A thermometer can measure the pine cone in degrees.
    B   A beaker can measure the pine cone in milliliters.
    C   A ruler can measure the pine cone in inches.
    D   A balance can measure the pine cone in grams.

    S4.A
    2.2.1

*This question asks for the instrument used by scientists to measure mass. The best answer is **Choice D**. A balance measures mass. Grams are also units of mass. The other answers are all incorrect. A thermometer measures temperature. A beaker measures volume. A ruler measures length or distance.*

Now answer some questions on your own. Circle the correct answer.

2. Five milliliters (5 mL) of additional water is added to the water in the beaker shown on the right. What is the total volume of the liquid in the beaker after this water is added?

    A   27 mL
    B   30 mL
    C   35 mL
    D   40 mL

    S4.A 2.2.1

3. A scientist wants to observe the changes in plants kept in rooms at different temperatures. Which tool would the scientist use to measure the temperature in each room?

    A   a microscope
    B   a thermometer
    C   a spring scale
    D   a double-pan balance

    ◆ **Examine the Question**
    ◆ **Recall What You Know**
    ◆ **Apply What You Know**

    S4.A 2.2.1

4. What units should a scientist use for measuring the mass of a soccer ball?

    A   kilometers
    B   degrees Celsius
    C   millimeters
    D   grams

    S4.A 2.2.1

5. A scientist puts a stick in the ground of his backyard. The height of the stick is one foot. For the next six months, he records the length of its shadow everyday exactly at noon. What variable is the scientist testing?

    A   the time of day
    B   the time of year
    C   the wind speed
    D   the outside temperature

    S4.A 2.1.2

6. In the diagram to the right, both the ruler and the plant are drawn to the same scale. Which measurement is closest to the height of the plant?

A   2½ inches
B   4 inches
C   5 inches
D   10 inches

S4.A
2.1.3

◆ Examine the Question
◆ Recall What You Know
◆ Apply What You Know

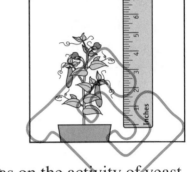

7. Kara did an experiment to find out what effects heat has on the activity of yeast. Which of these steps should come **last** in her experiment?

A   Add 1 gram of yeast to each bowl.
B   Observe what happens in each bowl.
C   Put 10 ounces of water in each bowl.
D   Move one bowl with yeast to a warmer location.

S4.A
2.1.2

8. Which tool is the **best** instrument for a scientist to use to measure the volume of water poured on a plant stem each morning?

A   a ruler
B   a thermometer
C   a microscope
D   a beaker

S4.A
2.2.1

9. Three friends want to see who can throw a Frisbee the farthest. Each person throws a Frisbee in the same direction and from the same place. However, each person throws a Frisbee that is different in size, shape and weight. How can the investigation be improved to provide fairer results?

A   Everyone should throw the Frisbee at the same time.
B   Everyone should throw a Frisbee with a similar shape.
C   Everyone should throw the same Frisbee.
D   Everyone should throw a Frisbee of the same color.

S4.A
2.1.2

10. A scientist is studying water evaporation. Which two measurements could she use to see how quickly a bowl of water evaporated?

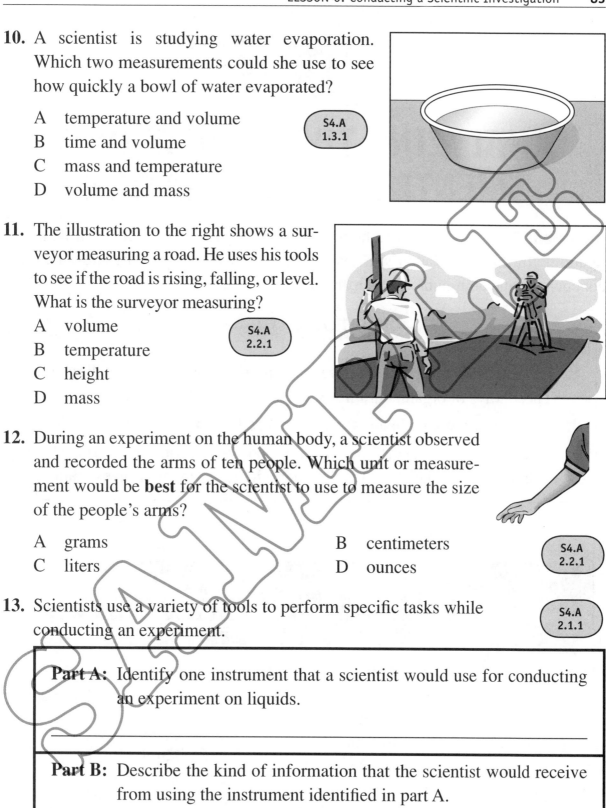

S4.A
1.3.1

A   temperature and volume
B   time and volume
C   mass and temperature
D   volume and mass

11. The illustration to the right shows a surveyor measuring a road. He uses his tools to see if the road is rising, falling, or level. What is the surveyor measuring?

A   volume
B   temperature
C   height
D   mass

S4.A
2.2.1

12. During an experiment on the human body, a scientist observed and recorded the arms of ten people. Which unit or measurement would be **best** for the scientist to use to measure the size of the people's arms?

A   grams
C   liters

B   centimeters
D   ounces

S4.A
2.2.1

13. Scientists use a variety of tools to perform specific tasks while conducting an experiment.

S4.A
2.1.1

Part A: Identify one instrument that a scientist would use for conducting an experiment on liquids.

_____

Part B: Describe the kind of information that the scientist would receive from using the instrument identified in part A.

_____

_____

ANALYZING THE RESULTS OF A SCIENTIFIC INVESTIGATION

In **Lessons 5** and **6**, you learned how scientists design and conduct scientific investigations. In this lesson, you will learn how scientists interpret their results, draw conclusions and communicate their findings.

— IMPORTANT IDEAS —

A. Scientists often organize their results into **graphs**, **tables**, and **diagrams**. These ways of organizing information often reveal patterns in the data.

B. Scientists **draw conclusions** and **make predictions** based on their results.

C. Scientists communicate their results and conclusions to others. Other scientists should be able to repeat the same experiment or investigation.

ORGANIZING AND ANALYZING DATA

Once scientists make observations or take measurements, they record their results. Then they look to see if there are any patterns. To help them find these patterns, scientists often organize their results in the form of a table, graph, or diagram.

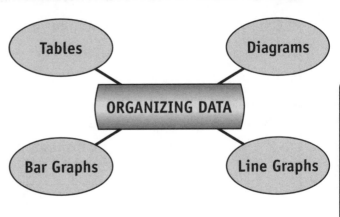

Tables — Diagrams — ORGANIZING DATA — Bar Graphs — Line Graphs

TABLES

Tables list information in columns and rows. To interpret a table, you need to pay close attention to its headings. A scientific table often shows the relationship between two variables. For example, look at the table below. It is based on the experiment with paper airplanes discussed in **Lesson 5**. This table shows each type of paper airplane and how far it has flown:

Type of Airplane	Distance Airplane Flew			
	Trial 1	Trial 2	Trial 3	Trial 4
"Flat-Nosed" Airplane	12 feet	15 feet	12 feet	9 feet
"Pointy-Nosed" Airplane	18 feet	15 feet	21 feet	18 feet

APPLYING WHAT YOU HAVE LEARNED

★ What distance did the flat-nosed airplane fly on its second trial? _____

★ What was the **average distance** flown by the pointy-nosed airplane? (*To find the average, simply add together all the distances. Then divide their sum by 4, the number of trials.*) _____

★ What conclusion can you draw from this data? _____

_____

_____

BAR GRAPHS

A **bar graph** is made up of bars of different lengths. Each bar represents a quantity of something. Each bar is labeled or a key is provided to tell what each bar represents. Look at the bar graph on the right.

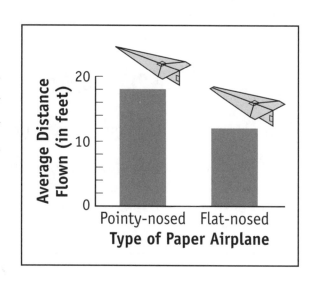

This graph shows the **average distance** flown by each of the two types of paper airplanes — the pointy-nosed and flat-nosed airplane over the four trials. These averages are based on the distances shown on the table on the prior page.

APPLYING WHAT YOU HAVE LEARNED

★ What was the average distance flown by the flat-nosed airplane? _____

★ Which of the airplanes flew a greater average distance? _____

★ How does information in a bar graph differ from a table? _____

_____

_____

LINE GRAPHS

A **line graph** shows a series of connected points on graph paper or a similar grid. Each point on the grid represents an amount. A line graph is usually labeled along its bottom line and left side. Carefully examine the key and the graph on the right.

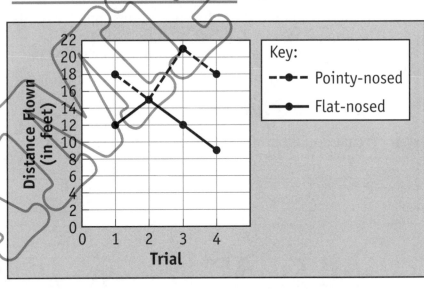

APPLYING WHAT YOU HAVE LEARNED

★ How far did the pointy-nosed airplane fly on trial 4? _____

★ How does a line graph differ from a table? _____

_____

_____

Usually a line graph is used to show how something **changes** over time, or how changes in one variable affect another variable.

Examine the line graph to the right. It shows how the temperature of the ocean changed as scientists went deeper into the water. Remember that a meter is about a yard in length.

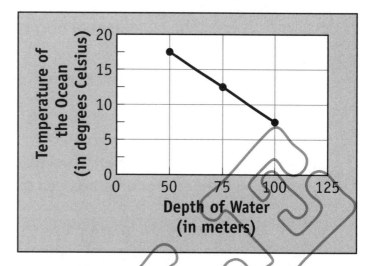

APPLYING WHAT YOU HAVE LEARNED

★ What is the temperature of the water at 75 meters deep? _____

★ How do these two variables seem to relate to each other? _____

_____

_____

_____

In a line graph, it is sometimes possible to guess at missing variables. Just look at the pattern in the graph above.

★ What do you think the ocean temperature is at 60 meters deep? _____

★ What do you think the ocean temperature is at 125 meters deep? _____

DIAGRAMS

Charts and diagrams can take many different forms. Most use pictures to show how things relate to one another. Lines or arrows often indicate relationships. For example, a group of scientists has investigated prairie animals. They have observed what those animals eat and recorded their observations. The diagram on the next page summarizes their findings:

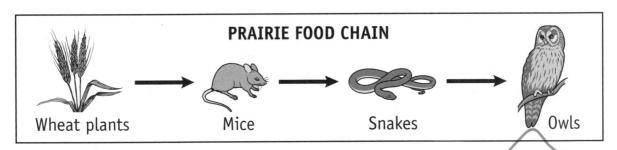

PRAIRIE FOOD CHAIN

Wheat plants → Mice → Snakes → Owls

This diagram shows that mice eat wheat plants for food. Snakes then eat the mice. The diagram shows the relationships between these prairie plants and animals.

APPLYING WHAT YOU HAVE LEARNED

★ What do mice eat for food on the prairie? _____

★ Which prairie animal eats snakes for food? _____

DRAWING CONCLUSIONS

After scientists organize the data from an experiment or investigation, they draw conclusions. **Conclusions** should be **consistent** with the data or observations from the investigation. That means that if the evidence from the experiment or field investigation does not support a conclusion, then the conclusion must be changed.

The most important conclusion usually concerns the **hypothesis** the scientists are testing:

★ Do the results of the investigation show that the hypothesis is correct or incorrect?

★ Do the results suggest how the hypothesis might be changed, or do they suggest a new hypothesis?

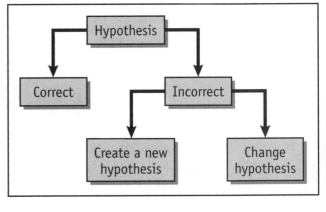

In addition to proving or disproving the hypothesis, scientists find they can often make new generalizations or predictions based on their results.

MAKING GENERALIZATIONS

A **generalization** is a general statement that summarizes what several pieces of data show. For example, examine the graph to the right. This is the same graph you examined previously on page 87. From this data, scientists might generalize that as you go deeper into the ocean, the temperature of the water becomes colder.

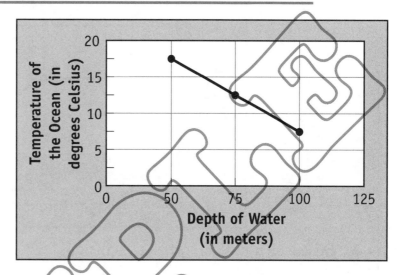

APPLYING WHAT YOU HAVE LEARNED

★ Give examples showing how this **generalization** is true for ocean depths from 50 to 100 meters: _____

_____

MAKING PREDICTIONS

Scientists often make predictions from the data. A **prediction** states what will probably happen in the future. For example, you have seen that as the ocean becomes deeper, its temperature becomes colder. Based on this generalization, you can predict the ocean temperature will be lower at 125 meters than at 100 meters. You might even guess that the temperature at this depth is likely to be around 3°C.

Based on the information in the graph, what do you think the temperature of the ocean will be at a depth of 65 meters? This temperature should be **lower** than the temperature at 50 meters, but **higher** than the temperature at 75 meters.

APPLYING WHAT YOU HAVE LEARNED

A scientist conducted an experiment growing nine bean plants in different amounts of light. The results of the experiment are shown in the line graph:

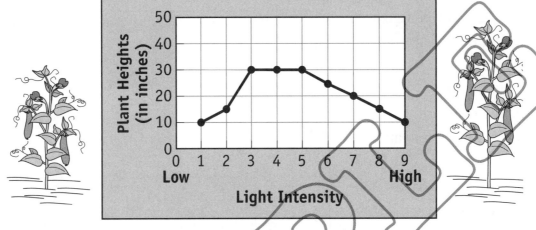

★ Based on the data, what conclusions can the scientist draw from this experiment? _____

_____

COMMUNICATING RESULTS

Once scientists complete an investigation, they must communicate their results to others. There are a variety of ways in which scientific findings can be reported. Usually this takes place in the form of a *written report, article,* or an *oral presentation.* A good presentation uses clear language and provides accurate data.

The presentation or written report must include the procedures followed by the scientist. This is done so that other scientists can *repeat*

Good scientists communicate their results to other scientists.

the experiment and see if they obtain the same results. Scientists may also include photographs or diagrams showing what steps they performed and displaying their results.

It is important to keep the conditions the same when repeating an experiment. If other scientists repeat the experiment but do not keep all the conditions the same, they may reach different results.

APPLYING WHAT YOU HAVE LEARNED

Scientist A placed two bean plants by the window in June. She watered each plant the same amount every day. She also gave one plant fertilizer, but did not fertilize the other plant. After one month, the plant with fertilizer grew 12 cm. The plant without fertilizer grew only 6 cm. The scientist concluded that giving bean plants fertilizer increases their growth. Scientist B decided to repeat the experiment. In December, he placed two plants by the window. He watered each plant the same amount. He gave no fertilizer to the second plant. After one month, the first plant had grown 6 cm in height, and the second plant had grown 3 cm in height.

★ Why did Scientist B arrive at different results from Scientist A in this experiment? _____

_____

★ Why are comparisons of results from different experiments unfair when not all of the experimental conditions are the same? _____

_____

WHAT YOU SHOULD KNOW

☐ You should know that scientists organize and analyze data by making tables, graphs, and diagrams. You should be able to interpret each of these.

☐ You should know how to draw conclusions and make predictions from the results of an investigation.

- To make a generalization, look at the data and decide what it shows.
- To make a prediction, guess what will happen based on patterns in the data.

☐ You should know that scientists communicate their results and conclusions to others. Other scientists should be able to repeat the experiment and reach similar results.

LESSON STUDY CARDS

Analyzing Data

★ **Ways of Displaying Data**
- **Table.** Gives information in columns and rows to make large amounts of information easier to read.
- **Bar Graph.** Shows data in columns to make comparisons easier among the data
- **Line Graph.** Shows data as a series of connected points, making it easier to see trends between two or more items.
- **Diagram.** Represents the data as a picture, making it easier to understand.

Drawing Conclusions

★ The experiment should prove or disprove the hypothesis. The results may suggest ways to change the hypothesis for further testing.

- **Generalization.** Describes what the data shows.
- **Prediction.** States what the data would be in a new situation, based on patterns in the existing data.

★ Conclusions should always be consistent with what the data or information shows.

CHECKING YOUR UNDERSTANDING

1. Scientists combine two chemicals in water. The chart to the right shows the temperature of the mixture during the first five minutes after the chemicals are mixed. Which statement **best** predicts the temperature after six minutes?

A It will decrease.
B It will remain the same.
C It will increase to 200°C
D It will increase to 600°C

S4.A 2.1.4

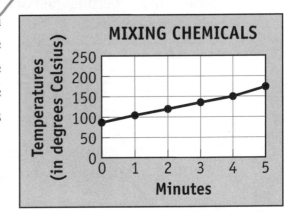

MIXING CHEMICALS

HINT *This question asks you to state a conclusion that is consistent with the data. The data shows a steady increase in the temperature of the mixture. Based on this trend, the mixture should continue to increase in temperature over the next minute to about 200°C. Thus, the correct answer is **C**.*

Now answer some questions on your own. Circle the correct answer.

Use the table below to answer question 2.

Temperature (°C)	Days Needed for Seeds to Sprout
25	5
20	7
15	9
10	11
5	?

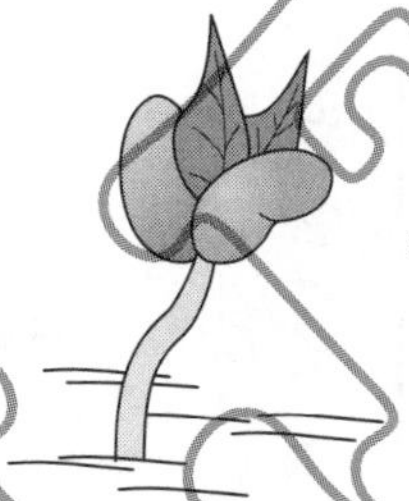

2. The above chart shows the time it took for bean seeds to sprout at different temperatures. Based on this data, when will seeds at 5°C most likely sprout?

   A   5 days
   B   8 days
   C   13 days
   D   16 days

   ♦ **Examine the Question**
   ♦ **Recall What You Know**
   ♦ **Apply What You Know**

   S4.A 1.3.3

3. A scientist measures the lengths of 100 tadpoles from two different ponds. She then calculates the average tadpole length in each pond and finds they are almost the same. What conclusion is most consistent with this data?

   A   One pond receives more sunlight than the other pond.
   B   Conditions in the two ponds are very similar.
   C   One pond has more insects than the other pond.
   D   Tadpoles in both ponds are eaten by the fish.

   S4.A 2.1.4

4. Which question would be most testable in a scientific investigation?

   A   Do dogs make better pets than cats?
   B   Are dogs happy when they are taken for a walk?
   C   Do dogs sleep more than human beings?
   D   Are cats easier to take care of than dogs?

   S4.A 2.1.1

Use the graph below to answer questions 5 and 6.

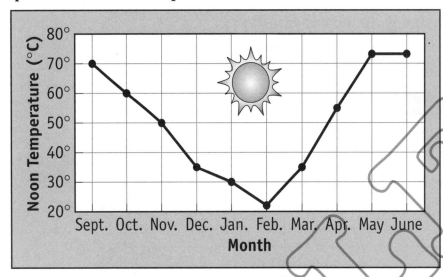

5. A class recorded the outdoor temperature at noon on the first day of the month for an entire school year. The graph above shows their results. What was the temperature on the first day of March?

    A   30°C   B   35°C

    C   40°C   D   75°C

    ◆ Examine the Question
    ◆ Recall What You Know
    ◆ Apply What You Know

    S4.A
    2.1.3

6. From October to January, what happened to the temperature?

    A   It decreased.
    B   It increased.
    C   It remained the same.
    D   It decreased then increased.

    S4.A
    2.1.4

7. A tropical plant that usually lives in a shady rainforest grew inside a house during the winter months. In spring, it was placed outside in full sunlight. The leaves of the plant soon died. Which statement is a correct conclusion about this event?

    A   The plant learned to stay healthy.
    B   The plant adapted well to sunlight.
    C   The plant was negatively affected by the bright sunlight.
    D   The plant could shed its leaves at any time.

    S4.A
    1.3.3

Use the bar graph below to answer question 8.

8.   The bar graph shows the height of a plant over a four-week period. According to the graph, how many additional inches did the plant grow from Week 2 to Week 4?

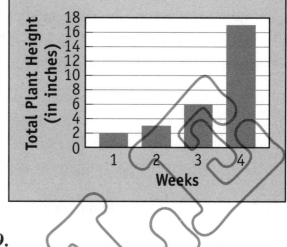

   A   6 inches

   B   10 inches

   C   14 inches

   D   17 inches

S4.A
1.3.1

Use the graph below to answer question 9.

9.   Scientists conducted an experiment to see how the design of a paper airplane affects the distance it can fly. The graph indicates the results of their experiment. It compares two paper airplane designs — a pointy-nosed and a flat-nosed paper airplane.

S4.A
2.1.4
2.1.1

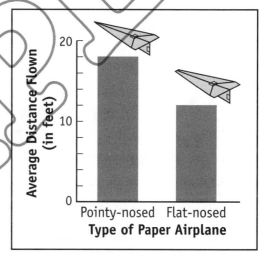

Part A: State one conclusion about the results of this experiment.

_____

_____

Part B: Identify one new question that scientists might investigate, based on the results of this experiment.

_____

_____

10. Scientist A put seeds in a pot of soil. He watered the seeds and put the pot next to a window. Scientist B put the same type of seeds in a pot of soil and watered them. She put the pot inside a box and covered its lid. She then placed the box next to a window. After one month, Scientist A's seeds grew into plants. Scientist B's seeds did not. What is the **best** conclusion to draw from these results?

A   Scientist B's seeds were too warm to grow.
B   Scientist B needed to use better soil.
C   Scientist B's seeds did not get enough sunlight.
D   Scientist A's pot helped his seeds to grow.

S4.A
2.1.4

11. Scientists conducted an experiment to see the effect of fire on a piece of wood. The illustration below shows the wood before and after it was set on fire.

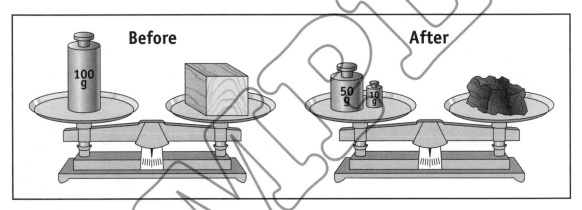

Part A: Complete the chart showing the mass of the wood before and after it was set on fire.

S4.A
2.1.1

	Before	After	Amount of Change
Mass of the wood *(in grams)*			

Part B: Describe a conclusion that a scientist could reach from this experiment.

S4.A
2.1.4

_____

_____

_____

LESSON 8

SCIENCE AND TECHNOLOGY

In this lesson, you will learn about technology and its impact.

— IMPORTANT IDEAS —

A. **Technology** is the use of tools, materials, processes and systems to solve problems and provide benefits. Technology and science are closely related.

B. Throughout history, technology has changed and improved. Modern technology includes physical technology, informational technology and biotechnology.

C. Changes in technology have had both **positive** and **negative impacts**.

WHAT IS TECHNOLOGY?

Technology is the use of tools, processes and systems by people to solve their problems and to provide benefits. Technology is as old as human-kind itself. During the Stone Age, people made tools of wood, stone, or bones to meet their needs. For example, early humans made arrowheads by chipping the sides of stones. They attached these arrowheads to sticks of wood. They used animal fibers and curved sticks to make bows. They used these bows and arrows to hunt animals for food or to fight against one another.

The first humans made arrows by sharpening stones.

With the introduction of **agriculture** (*farming*), human technology became more complex. People learned to plant seeds to grow food. They used new tools to break up the soil, to spread seeds, and to bring in the harvest. People could then stay in one place, so they built permanent homes and towns.

Next, people developed the first cities and systems of writing. They invented wheels and sailboats. They also learned how to make objects of metal. Technology slowly improved until the 1700s, when it advanced rapidly with the start of the **Industrial Revolution**. People began making goods in factories with machines. Steam power and electricity further changed people's lives. Western Pennsylvania became a center of the iron and steel industry. This area produced the steel for America's tools, factories and railroads. Today, we continue to live in an age of rapid technological change.

MODERN TECHNOLOGY

Today, modern technology covers many important areas:

PHYSICAL TECHNOLOGY

Physical technology concerns methods of construction, manufacturing, and transportation. Its tools, processes and systems help us to build homes, schools, hospitals, roads and factories. Physical technology also helps us to manufacture goods like clothing and cars.

Ford Motor Plant: 1900

Ford Motor Plant: 2000

APPLYING WHAT YOU HAVE LEARNED

Both pictures on the previous page were taken inside the Ford Motor Company plant. They show workers assembling automobiles. The time span between these pictures is 100 years. How have improvements in technology led to changes in the ways cars are made?

_____

_____

_____

INFORMATION TECHNOLOGY

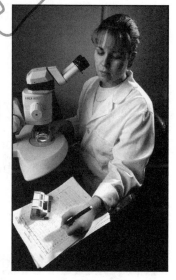

Information technology includes methods for encoding, storing, sending, receiving, and displaying information. Information technology makes it possible for us to have telephones, televisions, computers, digital cameras, cell phones, and the Internet.

BIOTECHNOLOGY

Biotechnology involves processes with living things. Biotechnology uses plants, animals and microscopic living things to produce things, such as drugs or materials to convert waste. Biotechnology affects health care, farming, and waste treatment.

THE IMPACT OF TECHNOLOGY

Like science, technology is constantly changing and improving. These changes come from people developing new ways of doing things. For example, people living in your area once moved on foot or by canoe. The arrival of new settlers brought the horse-drawn cart. Later, the invention of the steam engine led to the steamboat and railroad. In the early 1900s, the development of a new type of engine led to the car and airplane.

Today, people in your community have many ways to travel. They can travel on foot or by bicycle, motorcycle, car or bus. Some even travel by jet airplane.

These rapid changes in technology have had both positive and negative impacts on human society and the natural environment.

POSITIVE IMPACTS

Many new technologies have greatly improved people's lives.

AGRICULTURE

Some of the most important early inventions were in agriculture. In more recent times, improvements in technology, like the introduction of tractors and pesticides, have enabled farmers to grow more food with less effort.

Wheat harvested by an early mechanical reaper.

TRANSPORTATION

Since the 1800s, transportation has been greatly improved by such technological advances as the steamboat, train, automobile, and airplane. These improvements have made it easier for people to move around and to ship goods and materials.

MANUFACTURING

Starting in the 1700s, new technology helped people increase their ability to manufacture goods. Using large, powerful machines powered by steam, manufacturers produced vast amounts of cloth. These same technologies were gradually applied to producing every type of good — from clothes to cars. Manufacturers began using new types of energy, like electricity.

COMMUNICATIONS

The printing press, radio, telephone, television, and Internet have greatly improved people's ability to communicate. A person in one part of the world can now instantly communicate with someone else in almost any other part of the world.

ENERGY PRODUCTION

Improvements in agriculture, manufacturing, transportation and communications have required new sources of energy. In the 1700s and 1800s, people moved from human and water power to burning coal to make steam and electric power. In the early 1900s, people began using oil to make gasoline for cars and trucks. In the 1940s, nuclear power was introduced. These new sources of energy make it possible for us to light and heat our homes, to travel to distant places, and to manufacture goods in factories.

As the demand for energy rises, the search for more oil continues.

NEGATIVE IMPACTS

Technology is not always beneficial. Technological changes have had negative as well as positive effects on both society and the environment.

THE NATURE OF WORK

Improvements in technology changed the nature of work. Most people once worked on farms or in traditional crafts. Now many of them have been replaced by faceless machines. Other people face boring jobs in which they have no chance for creativity. Changes in the nature of work affect families as well as individuals. At one time, most members of the same family lived and worked together. After 1800, many began working outside the home in factories and other workplaces. As a result, family members spend much less time together.

THREATS TO THE ENVIRONMENT

Technology also now threatens Earth's environment. Improvements in agriculture, nutrition and health care have led to an explosion of the world's human population. People are using more and more of Earth's resources — air, water, and space. People's solid and liquid wastes are polluting our soil and water. The use of new **packaging materials** — such as plastic to wrap items — has created enormous amounts of garbage. Plastic packaging materials often will not dissolve in landfills, or wherever they are dumped.

The use of coal and oil as sources of energy also now threaten the environment. People pollute the atmosphere by burning coal and oil to power their cars and factories, to make electricity, and to heat their offices and homes. Pollution has increased the amount of carbon dioxide in the atmosphere. This has brought about "**global warming**."

Heat becomes trapped by the atmosphere. Temperatures on Earth's surface are rising, causing changes in climate. Some areas have less rainfall, while others have more hurricanes, floods and tidal waves.

Factories today often threaten the environment.

While technology has caused many problems, it is also contributing to their solution. Scientists study and develop new sources of clean energy and ways of saving the environment.

WARFARE

Technology has also increased human destructiveness. In prehistoric times, people attacked each other with spears and clubs. In the ancient world, improvements in the use of metals led to the invention of swords. Later, the development of gunpowder led to the use of cannons and guns. Each new weapon has been more destructive than previous ones. In 1945 the first atomic bomb was exploded. Atomic weapons have made warfare much more dangerous and destructive. Atomic energy, if used in warfare, threatens to destroy life on Earth.

The atomic bomb dropped on Hiroshima killed thousands of people.

APPLYING WHAT YOU HAVE LEARNED

★ Has the overall impact of technology on people's lives been more helpful

or harmful? _____ Explain your answer. _____

_____

_____

APPLYING WHAT YOU HAVE LEARNED

Everyday activities based on technology can affect the environment. For each example listed, identify how this human activity changes the environment. Then think of one way in which any negative effect on the environment could be reduced.

Human Activity	How this affects the environment	Ways to reduce any negative effects
Production of solid waste (garbage)		
Growing and eating of food		
Using water for drinking, farming, and manufacturing		
Transportation by land, water, and air		
Producing energy		

SCIENCE AND TECHNOLOGY

Science is driven by a desire to understand the natural world. **Technology** is driven by a desire to meet human needs. In fact, science and technology are closely related. Scientists rely on tools developed by technology, such as telescopes, microscopes, and thermometers. As the level of technology improves and introduces new products — like electricity, plastics, and computers — scientists are able to use many of these new tools for their own research.

Technology in turn relies on scientific discoveries. Our scientific understanding of the natural world guides the development of technology. Scientists developed the first electrical generators, x-rays, microwaves, antibiotics, jet engines, and nuclear energy. These discoveries became the basis for later inventions and technologies that we use today.

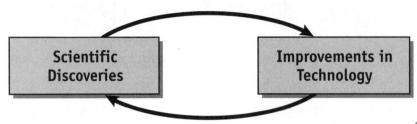

Developments in science and technology reinforce each other.

APPLYING WHAT YOU HAVE LEARNED

★ How are science and technology alike and different?

- Similarities. _____

_____

- Differences. _____

_____

★ Provide an example of a new technology based on a scientific discovery:

_____

★ Provide an example of a scientific discovery based on improvements in technology: _____

_____

WHAT YOU SHOULD KNOW

☐ You should know that technology is the use of tools, materials, processes, and systems to help meet human needs.

☐ You should know that there are physical technologies, informational technologies, and biotechnologies.

☐ You should know that changes in energy production, transportation, agriculture, communications, and packaging materials have had both positive and negative impacts on society and on the environment.

LESSON STUDY CARDS

The Impact of Technology

★ **Technology** is the use of tools, materials, processes and systems to meet human needs.

★ **Impact of Technology.** Technology can have both positive and negative impacts.

 • **Positive.** Improvements in energy production, transportation, communication, agriculture, and packaging materials.

 • **Negative.** Some jobs are monotonous; the environment is threatened by pollution; packaging materials add to pollution and waste; new weapons are very destructive.

Science and Technology

★ **Science.** Driven by a desire to understand the natural world.

★ **Technology.** Driven by a desire to meet human needs.

★ **Science and Technology.** Both reinforce each other, and are closely related.

 • Scientists rely on tools developed by technology.

 • Technology relies on scientific discoveries.

CHECKING YOUR UNDERSTANDING

1. Which technological change made it easier for people to move from one place to another?

    A   the invention of the railroad
    B   the creation of the first factories
    C   the invention of plastic
    D   the discovery of new rivers

    S4.A
    1.1.2

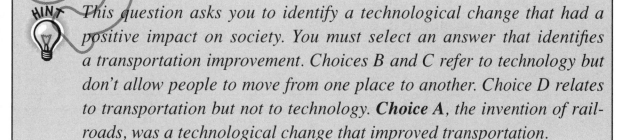

HINT *This question asks you to identify a technological change that had a positive impact on society. You must select an answer that identifies a transportation improvement. Choices B and C refer to technology but don't allow people to move from one place to another. Choice D relates to transportation but not to technology. **Choice A**, the invention of railroads, was a technological change that improved transportation.*

Now answer some questions on your own. Circle the correct answer.

2. Which of the following has been a negative impact of technology?

A   Farmers are able to grow more food.

B   Increased pollution has led to global warming.

C   People enjoy music on the radio and CDs.

D   People can easily communicate around the globe.

S4.A
1.1.2

3. Which is a positive impact of the invention of the electric dishwasher?

A   It saves people time and effort.

B   It uses hot water to wash dishes.

C   It uses detergents that pollute the environment.

D   It uses more electricity than washing dishes by hand.

S4.A
1.1.2

4. A manufacturer invents a new type of plastic. When used for packaging, this new plastic keeps foods very fresh. What possible risk does this plastic present to the environment?

A   People will overeat if food can be stored and kept fresh.

B   The plastic may not dissolve in land-fill sites.

C   The color of the plastic is unattractive to many people.

D   The cost of manufacturing the plastic is very expensive.

S4.A
1.1.2

5. Technology can have both positive and negative impacts on our environment or society.

S4.A
1.1.2

Part A: Give one example of a past or recent technological change.

_____

_____

Part B: Identify a positive or negative impact of the technological change you identified in part A.

_____

_____

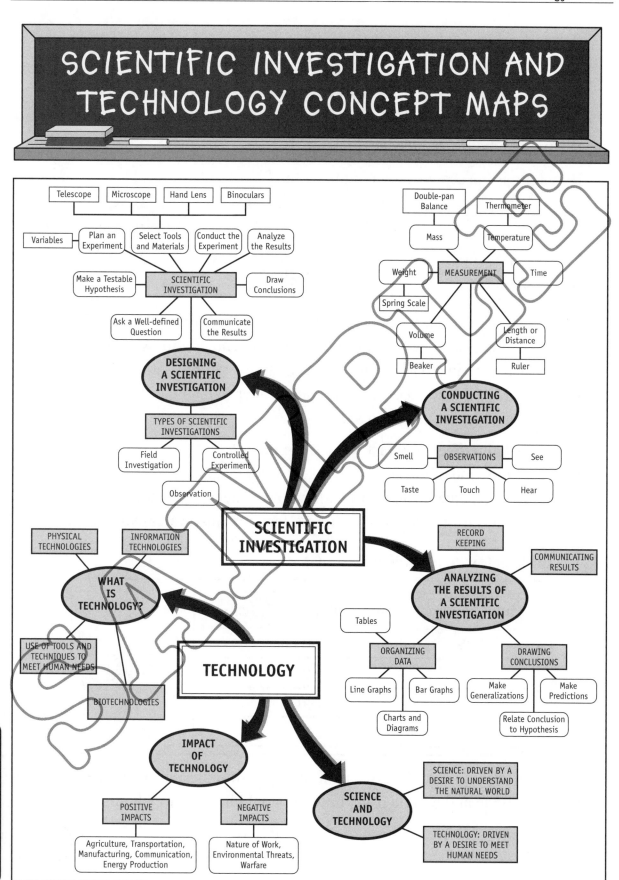

SCIENTIFIC INVESTIGATION AND TECHNOLOGY CONCEPT MAPS

TESTING YOUR UNDERSTANDING

Use the picture below to answer question 1.

1. How long is the screw shown in the picture?

    A   4 centimeters
    B   5 centimeters
    C   6 centimeters
    D   7 centimeters

    S4.A
    2.2.1

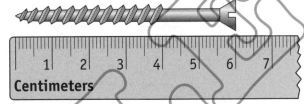

Centimeters

2. A student conducts an experiment. She fills two beakers with 200 mL of water. One beaker is placed in a dark room where the temperature is 68°F. The second beaker is placed in a dark room where the temperature is 50°F. Six hours later, she measures the amount of water in each beaker. Which question **best** describes what the student was trying to answer?

    A   Does light affect how fast water evaporates?
    B   Does the time of day affect how fast water evaporates?
    C   Does a container's shape affect how fast water evaporates?
    D   Does the surrounding temperature affect how fast water evaporates?

    S4.A
    2.1.1

Use the table below to answer question 3.

Time Traveled	Total Distance Traveled
2 hours	40 cm
4 hours	80 cm
6 hours	120 cm
8 hours	?

3. The table shows a snail's movement during a six-hour period. If the snail continues to move at the same pace, how far would it travel in 8 hours?

    A   40 cm
    C   120 cm

    B   160 cm
    D   180 cm

    S4.A
    2.1.3

4. Which question can **best** be answered through a scientific investigation?

    A   Why do people eat more apples than oranges?

    B   Does soup tastes better with salt?

    C   Does sound travel faster through water than air?

    D   How many designs are there for paper airplanes?

    S4.A
    2.1.1

5. Which of the following statements is an opinion?

    A   An asteroid will crash into Earth soon.

    B   The moon has both day and night.

    C   Earth orbits the sun once every 365 days.

    D   Stars are made up of super-heated gases.

    S4.A
    1.1.1

Use the table below to answer question 6.

Day	Monday	Tuesday	Wednesday	Thursday	Friday
Temperature	72°F	77°F	78°F	82°F	70°F

6. The table shows data recorded by students in Pittsburgh from Monday to Friday. Which thermometer correctly shows the temperature recorded on Friday?

    S4.A
    2.2.1

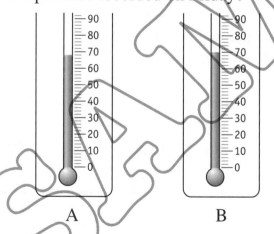
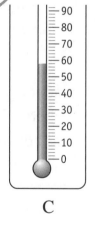
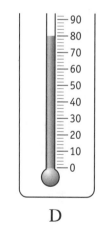

A   B   C   D

7. A scientist writes an article for a scientific journal describing an experiment he has conducted. Why is it important that the scientist clearly describes all of the steps he followed?

    A   Scientists often make predictions based on patterns in the data.

    B   Comparisons between experiments are often unfair.

    C   Scientists should be able to repeat the experiment.

    D   His conclusions should either prove or disprove his hypothesis.

    S4.A
    2.1.2

8. A group of students watches a bird as it flies out of a tree. They also spot a nest in the same tree. How can they **best** find out if the bird lives in the nest?

    A   measure the size of the bird

    B   drop bread crumbs at the base of the tree

    C   observe the nest for several days

    D   move the nest to their classroom

(S4.A 2.1.2)

Use the table below to answer question 9.

Plant Group	Light per day (in hours)	Average growth in one week (in cm)
Group 1	4	1
Group 2	6	4
Group 3	8	6
Group 4	10	3

9. The table above shows the growth of different groups of plants placed in sunlight for different amounts of time. Which conclusion is most consistent with this data?

    A   Plants with 10 hours of sunlight a day grew the most.

    B   Plants with 4 hours of sunlight a day had the most leaves.

    C   Plants with 6 hours of sunlight a day had the thickest leaves.

    D   Plants with 8 hours of sunlight a day grew the most.

(S4.A 2.1.4)

10. A group of students conducts an experiment in their science class. They add salt to two beakers of water. They have two beakers without salt. Then they record how long it takes water to evaporate from each beaker.

(S4.A 2.1.1 2.1.2)

Part A: What question are the students trying to answer? _____

_____

Part B: Identify one measurement the students should take in this experiment.

_____

11. Which laboratory instrument can be used to measure the weight of a small stone?

A   beaker   B   meter stick

C   thermometer   D   spring scale

CHECKLIST OF ELIGIBLE CONTENT

Directions. Now that you have completed this unit, place a check (✔) next to the eligible content from those assessment anchors that you understand. If you are having trouble recalling information about any of these, review the bolded lesson in the brackets.

☐ **S4.A.1.1.2** Identify and describe examples of common technological changes past to present in the community (e.g., energy production, transportation, communications, agriculture, packaging materials) that have either positive or negative impacts on society or the environment. [**Lesson 8**]

☐ **S4.A.1.3.1** Observe and record change by using time and measurement. [**Lesson 6**]

☐ **S4.A.1.3.3** Observe and describe the change to objects caused by temperature change or light [**Lesson 6**]

☐ **S4.A.2.1.1** Generate questions about objects, organisms, or events that can be answered through scientific investigations. [**Lesson 5**]

☐ **S4.A.2.1.2** Design and describe an investigation (a fair test) to test one variable. [**Lesson 5**]

☐ **S4.A.2.1.3** Observe a natural phenomenon (e.g., weather changes, length of daylight/night, movement of shadows, animal migrations, growth of plants), record observations, and then make a prediction based on those observations. [**Lesson 6**]

☐ **S4.A.2.1.4** State a conclusion that is consistent with the information/data. [**Lesson 6**]

☐ **S4.A.2.2.1** Identify appropriate tools or instruments for specific tasks and describe the information they can provide (e.g., measuring length — ruler, mass — balance, weight — scale, volume — beaker, temperature — thermometer; making observations: hand lens, binoculars, telescope). [**Lesson 6**]

☐ **S4.A.3.3.2** Identify and describe observable patterns (e.g., growth patterns in plants, weather, water cycle). [**Lesson 7**]

UNIT 3 — BIOLOGICAL SCIENCES

In this unit, you will learn about living things — plants and animals. You will learn about their characteristics, their body parts, and their life cycles.

You will learn how some living things inherit some characteristics from their parents. You will also learn how they survive and interact in different environments.

Flamingos interacting with their environment

★ **Lesson 9: The Characteristics of Living Things.** In this lesson, you will learn the basic needs and processes of all living things. You will also learn how different parts of plants and animals work together to meet their needs, how organisms inherit characteristics from their parents, and how organisms have different life cycles.

★ **Lesson 10: Ecosystems.** In this lesson, you will learn how plants and animals interact with each other and their environment. You will also learn how human activities affect the environment.

KEY TERMS YOU WILL LEARN ABOUT IN THIS UNIT

- Life Process
- Growth
- Digestion
- Respiration
- Reproduction
- Photosynthesis
- Carbon Dioxide

- Leaves, stems, roots
- Adaptations
- Inherited Characteristics
- Life Cycles
- Metamorphosis
- Ecosystem
- Lentic System

- Lotic System
- Predators/Prey
- Producers
- Consumers
- Decomposers
- Food Chain
- Food Web

LESSON 9

THE CHARACTERISTICS OF LIVING THINGS

In this chapter, you will learn the main characteristics of plants and animals.

— IMPORTANT IDEAS —

A. All living things, or **organisms**, need air, water, food and shelter.

B. The different parts of an organism work together to meet its needs.

C. **Plants** are able to make their own food using energy from sunlight.

D. **Animals** are unable to make their own food. However, animals can move from one place to another. Their senses help to guide their movements.

E. **Adaptations** help organisms survive in their environment.

F. Each plant and animal has its own unique **life cycle**.

G. Plants and animals **inherit** many characteristics from their parents.

THE NEEDS OF LIVING THINGS

All living things, or **organisms**, have certain basic needs — such as air, water, food and shelter.

APPLYING WHAT YOU HAVE LEARNED

Describe how you go about meeting your needs for:

★ Air: _____

★ Food: _____

★ Water: _____

★ Shelter: _____

All organisms have special life processes to help them survive, grow and reproduce. These **life processes** include the following:

| **GROWTH** All living things need to grow. | **DIGESTION** All living things break down and absorb food. | **RESPIRATION** All animals absorb oxygen, which they use to burn food for energy. | **REPRODUCTION** All living things produce offspring. (*children*) |

Organisms have different characteristics to help them meet their basic needs and to carry on their life processes. Two types of living things with different characteristics are plants and animals.

APPLYING WHAT YOU HAVE LEARNED

★ Plants and animals exist all around you. List two characteristics you already know for plants and animals.

PLANTS	ANIMALS
• _____ _____ • _____	• _____ _____ • _____

Scientists have found some important differences between plants and animals. Let's examine some of these differences.

PLANTS

Most plants are green because they have a special chemical that helps them turn energy from sunlight into food. Unlike animals, plants cannot move on their own.

HOW PLANTS MEET THEIR NEEDS

Plants have three parts: their *leaves*, *stems*, and *roots*. Each part helps the plant meet its basic needs.

LEAVES

Leaves make food from the sun's energy. This process is called **photosynthesis**. Tiny pores (*openings*) in the bottom of the leaves let in **carbon dioxide**, a gas in the air. In the leaves, carbon dioxide and water are combined, using energy from sunlight, to produce a type of sugar. The plant uses this sugar as food. Photosynthesis also gives off oxygen. This oxygen is released into the air through the pores of leaves.

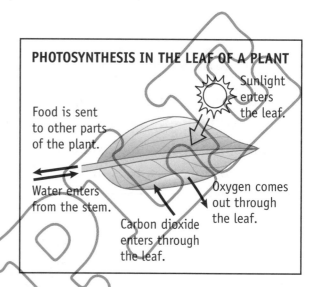

PHOTOSYNTHESIS IN THE LEAF OF A PLANT

Sunlight enters the leaf.

Food is sent to other parts of the plant.

Water enters from the stem.

Carbon dioxide enters through the leaf.

Oxygen comes out through the leaf.

STEMS

Stems are the main body of the plant. For example, the trunk of a tree is a very thick stem. Stems support a plant's leaves and flowers. Stems also move water and minerals to the leaves, and send food from the leaves to the roots.

ROOTS

A plant's roots are usually found below the ground. They hold the plant in place, and absorb water and minerals from the soil.

APPLYING WHAT YOU HAVE LEARNED

★ How do plants make their food? _____

_____

★ How do plants get their water? _____

_____

Adaptations. Over time, different types of plants have developed special characteristics to survive in their environment. These characteristics are known as **adaptations**. For example, a cactus has a thick stem to hold water. This helps it to live in dry climates. Other plants adapt to their environment by developing large leaves to catch more sunlight in shady environments like rain forests.

THE LIFE CYCLE OF PLANTS

Do you look the same as you did five years ago? Of course not! As you live, you change. All living things go through stages known as the **life cycle**. All organisms begin life, grow, age, and eventually die. As organisms age, they often go through important changes. Here is the typical life cycle of a flowering plant:

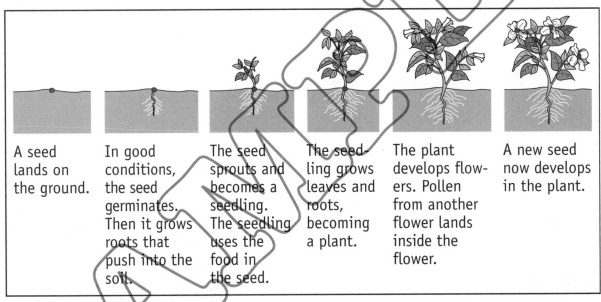

A seed lands on the ground.

In good conditions, the seed germinates. Then it grows roots that push into the soil.

The seed sprouts and becomes a seedling. The seedling uses the food in the seed.

The seedling grows leaves and roots, becoming a plant.

The plant develops flowers. Pollen from another flower lands inside the flower.

A new seed now develops in the plant.

Spreading Seeds. Plants cannot move around like animals can. Seeds need to move away from their parent plant to survive. Seeds that grow too close to their parent will compete with the parent for water and sunlight.

How do seeds move? Many seeds are blown by the wind. Some seeds stick to the fur of an animal, or float on water. Other seeds are found in fruits, which are eaten by animals. When the seeds are passed out or discarded by the animal, they grow in another place.

Seeds are carried in fruits (apples, bananas, tomatoes).

APPLYING WHAT YOU HAVE LEARNED

Carefully examine the illustration to the right. Number the different plants in the order of their development in the plant life cycle.

★ Step 1: _____

★ Step 2: _____

★ Step 3: _____

★ Step 4: _____

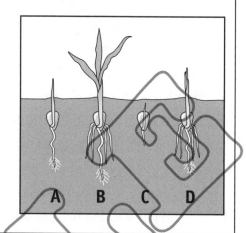

Like plants, animals also have special characteristics that help them to meet their basic needs. Unlike plants, animals cannot produce their own food. However, they can move from place to place to find food.

HOW ANIMALS MEET THEIR NEEDS

SENSE ORGANS

Animals have senses like touch, smell, taste, hearing and sight. These senses help animals to know when they are in danger and where they can find food.

MOVEMENT

All animals move. This permits them to find food and to hide or escape from their enemies. Animals have different structures to help them move. Fish have **fins** and **tails**, which help them to swim through the water. Birds and many insects have **wings**, which allow them to fly. Insects, birds, reptiles, and mammals have **legs**, which help them to walk on land.

BREATHING

Oxygen is a gas in the air that animals use to burn food. **Respiration** is the process by which animals get oxygen. Special structures help animals to obtain oxygen. Many land-based animals breathe oxygen from the air through their mouths and noses. The oxygen then goes to the lungs, where it enters the blood. Fish absorb dissolved oxygen in the water through their **gills**. All the parts of each animal's respiration system work together.

DRINKING AND EATING (DIGESTION)

Animals must have food and water to survive. Special structures, such as the **mouth**, allow animals to drink and eat. Food and water are then broken down and absorbed into the body in the **digestive process**. This process allows the animal to absorb needed nutrients and water. All the parts of the digestive system work together.

BODY COVERINGS

Most animals are covered by skin, scales, hair or feathers. The covering holds the body together, provides warmth, and protects the animal from outside conditions.

APPLYING WHAT YOU HAVE LEARNED

★ How do each of these senses help you meet your basic needs?

Sight:	
Smell:	
Hearing:	
Touch:	
Taste:	

DIFFERENT TYPES OF ANIMALS

Scientists classify animals into different types, based on their external characteristics:

Type	Lives on Land or Water	Body Covering	Segments or Skeleton	Limbs	Examples
Insects	Generally live on land or water.	Covered with tough outer layer called exoskeleton.	Three body segments: head, thorax (chest), and abdomen	Most have four wings and six legs.	Ants, flies, grasshoppers, bees, mosquitoes
Arachnids	Generally live on land.	Tough outer layer	Two body segments	Have eight legs.	Spiders, ticks, scorpions
Fish	Live in salt water or fresh water. Can't survive out of water.	Covered with scales.	Internal skeleton with bones.	Usually have no legs: have fins and tails.	Salmon, bass, trout, tuna
Amphibians	Amphibians begin life in the water. Most live on land as adults.	Smooth skin without scales.	Internal skeleton with bones.	Usually have four legs.	Frogs, toads, salamanders
Reptiles	Generally live on land and water.	Waterproof scales.	Internal skeleton with bones.	Usually have four legs, but some have none.	Alligators, snakes, turtles, lizards
Birds	Generally live on land.	Bodies are covered with feathers.	Internal skeleton with bones.	Front limbs are wings. Most are able to fly.	Chickens, eagles, ducks, cardinals
Mammals	Generally live on land. Whales, seals, and dolphins live in water.	Covered in skin with fur or hair.	Internal skeleton with bones.	Have four legs or two legs and two arms.	Zebras, monkeys, cats, dogs, humans

ADAPTATIONS

Every type of animal also has special adaptations that help it survive in its environment. For example, the color of an animal may blend with plants found in its environment. This **protective coloration** makes it harder for enemies to hunt for it. There are many other kinds of adaptations. For example, the hover fly resembles a honey bee. This **mimicry** keeps other animals from attacking it.

Some insects look like a stick or leaf, making it hard for enemies to see them.

Here are other examples of adaptations that help some animals to survive:

GIRAFFE

A giraffe's long neck and keen eyesight help it to see for many miles. Its long neck also helps it to eat tree leaves too high for most other animals. Scientists believe giraffes' skin patterns make them look like tall trees, hiding them from other animals.

ALLIGATORS

Alligators store fat that can be used in the winter. Alligators also have long tails, long snouts with noses on top, and scaly, bumpy skin. These characteristics help alligators to swim and hide. Alligators have small legs, so they can walk on land to lay eggs. They can live on land or in the water, which is perfect for the swamplands they inhabit.

CAMELS

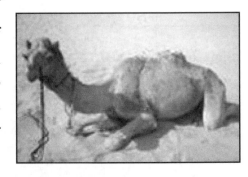

A camel is a large mammal with one or two humps of body fat. Camels store water in their blood and can live without water for two weeks. This helps them to survive in dry desert environments. Camels are able to withstand changes in body temperature. Their thick coat of camel hair reflects strong sunlight.

APPLYING WHAT YOU HAVE LEARNED

Every animal has characteristics that help it survive. Choose two animals. For each, identify a characteristic and tell how it helps this animal survive.

Animal	Special Characteristic

THE LIFE CYCLE OF ANIMALS

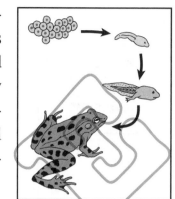

Like plants, animals also have their own **life cycles**. Reptiles, fish, insects, and birds are born from eggs. Mammals have live births. All animals then grow, reproduce, age and die. Some animals have special life cycles. They actually change form. For example, a frog begins life as an egg living in the water. The egg hatches as a **tadpole**. After several weeks, the tadpole develops tiny front and back legs. Eventually, the tadpole grows into a young frog.

Many insects go through a special process, known as **metamorphosis**. They completely change their form. For example, a butterfly lays an egg. Out of the egg

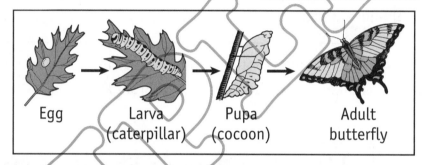

| Egg | Larva (caterpillar) | Pupa (cocoon) | Adult butterfly |

comes a worm-like **larva** (*or caterpillar*). The larva wraps itself up in a **pupa** (*or cocoon*). After a period of time, an **adult** butterfly with wings emerges from the pupa. Moths follow the same process.

However, not all insects have a complete metamorphosis. For example, baby grasshoppers (*nymphs*) look just like small adults without wings. Grasshoppers get larger in stages but do not change how they look very much.

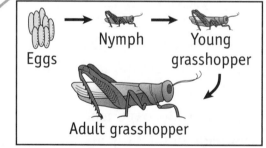

APPLYING WHAT YOU HAVE LEARNED

★ Describe each of the following stages in the life cycle of a frog:

Egg		
Tadpole		
Adult Frog		

APPLYING WHAT YOU HAVE LEARNED

★ How do plants and animals differ? Complete the blank boxes below.

Characteristic	Plants	Animals
Movement	Generally rooted in one place and cannot move on their own.	
Food		Cannot make their own food. Must eat plants or other animals.
Sense Organs	Have no sense organs.	

★ Choose one plant or animal that you know. On a separate sheet of paper, make a chart showing the different stages of its life cycle.

INHERITED CHARACTERISTICS

Organisms develop special behaviors in response to the environment. For example, you may get sunburned after being in the sun too long. After this experience, you learn to apply sunscreen lotion. Or you may learn to like pancakes with maple syrup. This is something you may have learned from other people.

Other characteristics you have are **inherited**. For example, your physical characteristics are inherited. Your height was inherited from your parents. So was the color of your eyes and hair. Inherited characteristics even include earlobes. Some people's earlobes are attached. Others are not. If both your parents' earlobes are attached, yours probably are too.

No matter how hard you try, you cannot change your height, the color of your eyes and hair or your earlobe type. Inherited characteristics are traits that cannot be changed.

APPLYING WHAT YOU HAVE LEARNED

Some people show dimples in their cheeks when they smile. Others, no matter how hard they try, cannot. When people put their hands together and interlock their fingers, they place either their left or right thumb on top. Other

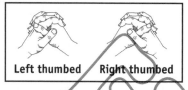

Left thumbed   Right thumbed

people can curl the sides of their tongue. Some people are able to make a "Vulcan" sign like Spock on Star Trek. These are all inherited traits. A person who cannot curl his or her tongue cannot learn to do so. Pick a classmate and list these easily observable traits. Compare your inherited traits with those of your partner:

Vulcan   Earthling

Characteristic	Your Trait	Classmate's Trait
1. Dimples when smiling	☐	☐
2. Right thumb on top	☐	☐
3. Able to curl tongue	☐	☐
4. "Vulcan" hand sign	☐	☐

WHAT YOU SHOULD KNOW

☐ You should know that all organisms need air, water, food and shelter to meet their basic needs. Different parts of each organism work together to help it meet its needs. Adaptations help organisms to survive their environment.

☐ You should know that plants have leaves, stems and roots. Plants are unable to move from one place to another. Plants are able to make their own food using the energy of sunlight.

☐ You should know that animals can move from place to place. They use senses to guide their movement. Scientists classify animals based on physical characteristics, such as their body segments, body coverings and limbs.

☐ You should know that plants and animals each have their own life cycles.

☐ You should know that organisms inherit many of their characteristics from their parents.

LESSON STUDY CARDS

Plants

★ Plants have three main parts:
- **Roots:** Anchor the plant in the ground.
- **Leaves:** Make food from the sun's energy.
- **Stems:** Support its leaves and flowers.

★ **Life Cycles:** First a seed; the seed sprouts; becomes a seedling; then a mature plant.

★ **Photosynthesis.** Plants make their own food out of sunlight through a process called photosynthesis.

★ Plants take in carbon dioxide and produce oxygen.

Animals

★ Animals cannot make their own food. They must eat plants or other animals.

★ Unlike plants, most animals can move from place to place to meet their needs.

★ Animals use their senses to guide their movements.

★ **Life Cycles.** Animals go through life cycles: birth, growth, reproduction, aging, and death. **Amphibians:** egg → tadpole → frog. **Metamorphosis:** an insect changes form: egg → larva → pupa → adult.

Processes of Organisms

★ **Basic Needs of Organisms:**
- Air
- Food
- Water
- Shelter

★ **Life Processes:**
- Growth
- Respiration
- Digestion
- Reproduction

★ **Parts of an Organism.** The parts of each living organism work together to meet the organism's needs.

Characteristics of Organisms

★ **Classifying Animals:** Animals can be classified based on their external characteristics.
- Body Segments or Internal Skeleton
- Body Covering: skin, scales, hair
- Limbs: wings, legs, arms

★ **Adaptations:** Plants and animals have special characteristics that help them to survive in their environment.

★ **Inherited Characteristics.** An organism inherits certain characteristics from its parents — like hair and eye color.

CHECKING YOUR UNDERSTANDING

 **1**

 **2**

 3

 4

1. Which is the correct order for the life cycle of this butterfly?

A 4 → 2 → 1 → 3

B 1 → 4 → 2 → 3

C 4 → 2 → 3 → 1

D 1 → 3 → 4 → 2

S4.B 1.1.5

HINT *To answer this question, you must recall the life cycle of a butterfly. A butterfly goes through a metamorphosis in its life cycle. When its egg hatches, a larva (caterpillar) comes out. The larva later becomes a pupa (cocoon). Out of the pupa comes an adult butterfly. The correct picture arrangement is 4 – 2 – 3 – 1.*

Now answer some other questions on your own. Circle the correct answer.

2. Owls eat mice and other small animals to survive. Owls hunt in the dark. Which of an owl's senses is most useful as it hunts?

    A taste   B touch

    C hearing   D sight

    S4.B
    2.1.1

3. Which is a characteristic that a student would learn from his parents?

    A his blue eyes   B his brown hair

    C his long, thin fingers   D his politeness to adults

    S4.B
    2.2.1

4. Which life process helps animals absorb oxygen from the air into their bodies?

    A growth
    B digestion
    C respiration
    D photosynthesis

    ◆ **Examine the Question**
    ◆ **Recall What You Know**
    ◆ **Apply What You Know**

    S4.B
    1.1.1

5. When cows graze on a field they often eat grass. What basic need do the cows meet by eating the grass?

    A water
    B shelter
    C food
    D air

    S4.B
    1.1.3

6. Which example describes a physical feature inherited from parents?

    A Mrs. Smith has brown eyes.
    B John talks very fast.
    C Dewayne runs to school.
    D Alice broke her wrist from a fall.

    S4.B
    2.2.1

Use the pictures below to answer question 7.

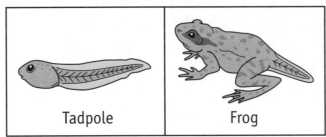

7.   Which example is **most** like the pair in the pictures?

A   caterpillar — butterfly

B   branch — tree

C   worm — snake

D   baby grasshopper — adult grasshopper

♦ Examine the Question
♦ Recall What You Know
♦ Apply What You Know

Use the pictures below to answer question 8.

Tree Branch

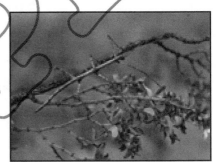

Stick insect in a tree

8.   A stick insect looks like a stick from a tree. Which statement **best** explains how this adaptation helps the stick insect to survive?

S4.B
2.1.2

A   It keeps other animals away from the stick insect's food.

B   It makes it hard for other animals to find the stick insect.

C   It helps the stick insect gather food from trees.

D   It protects the tree from other insects.

9.   The diagram to the right shows a bean seed in a container of soil. The first part to come out of the seed is labeled X. Which is a function of this part of the plant?

S4.B
1.1.4

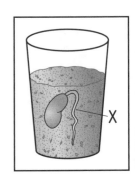

A   to make food

B   to produce other seeds

C   to absorb water

D   to release oxygen

10. The pictures below show the main stages in the life cycle of a fly. Which picture shows the life cycle of a fly in the right order?

S4.C
2.1.1

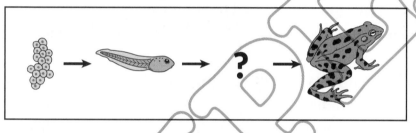

Use the picture below to answer question 11.

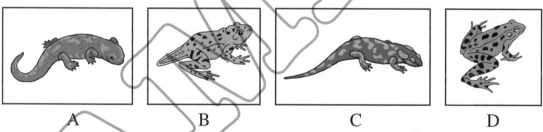

S4.B
1.1.5

11. Which stage of the frog's life cycle is missing from the picture above?

| A | B | C | D |

12. Plants and animals have many adaptations that help them survive.

Part A: Identify one special characteristic of a plant or animal you know that helps it to survive in its environment.

S4.B
2.1.1

_____

Part B: Explain how the characteristic you identified in part A helps that plant or animal survive.

S4.C
2.1.2

_____

LESSON 10

ECOSYSTEMS

In this lesson, you will learn how different types of living things survive and interact in ecosystems.

— IMPORTANT IDEAS —

A. An **ecosystem** is made up of all the living and nonliving things in an area. The living things in an ecosystem depend on both the living and nonliving parts of the ecosystem to survive.

B. Energy and nutrients are cycled through an ecosystem. Plants trap energy from the sun. Animals eat plants and other animals. Similar organisms in an ecosystem compete with each other for resources, such as oxygen, water, food or space.

C. Changes in the environment can cause changes among the organisms in an ecosystem.

D. Human activities affect the natural environment.

WHAT IS AN ECOSYSTEM?

Have you ever heard of an ecosystem? An **ecosystem** is made up of all the living and nonliving things in a particular area.

Every person, animal, plant, stream and area of land or water belongs to one or more ecosystems. Because they are in the same area, the living and nonliving parts of an ecosystem affect each other in different ways.

A pond's animals and plants form an ecosystem.

128

A small pond provides a good example of an **ecosystem**. The water, air, sunlight, and the mud at the bottom of the pond form the nonliving **physical environment** of the pond. The moss, pond grass, water lilies, and small green algae in or around the pond are forms of life that produce their own food. Insects, snails and other animals living in the pond eat some of these plants to survive. Fish eat the snails, insects and smaller fish in the pond. Frogs in the pond eat the insects found there.

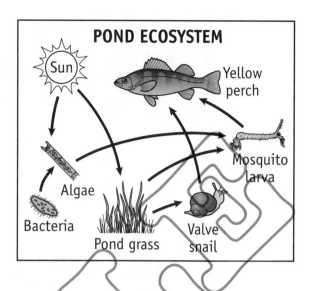

POND ECOSYSTEM

Sun

Algae

Bacteria

Pond grass

Yellow perch

Mosquito larva

Valve snail

Each of the living things in the pond has its own **habitat**, or special place. Algae grows in the water in the pond. Fish swim in the pond. Frogs jump around the surface of the pond. Each of these are habitats in this pond ecosystem. The fish, frogs, and insects all leave behind wastes. Snails, insects, fungi, and bacteria in and around the pond break down these wastes. Left undisturbed, a pond can continue to exist for many years. The different organisms in this pond ecosystem live in a **balanced relationship**.

APPLYING WHAT YOU HAVE LEARNED

★ How do the plants in a pond ecosystem depend on the nonliving environment to meet their basic needs? _____

_____

★ How do the animals in this ecosystem depend on other living things to meet their basic needs? _____

_____

★ What are some of the habitats of the animals in this pond ecosystem?

_____

_____

TYPES OF ECOSYSTEMS

The world has many different types of ecosystems. Each type of ecosystem is based on the characteristics of its nonliving environment, such as climate, how much water there is, and soil type. These characteristics help determine what kinds of plants and animals can live in that area.

LENTIC AND LOTIC SYSTEMS

A pond or lake is known as a **lentic system**. The water in a lentic system has no current. It is either still or moves very slowly. Algae and water plants make food from sunlight. Bacteria, fish, insects, and amphibians live in lentic ecosystems.

Is this wetland a lentic or lotic system?

A stream or river is known as a **lotic system**. The fresh water is constantly moving, and the water flows downwards. In a lotic ecosystem, living things must be able to live in flowing water. Many important conditions affect lotic systems. These include the speed at which the water flows, the amount of sunlight, and the average temperature. Algae, bacteria, plants, fish, insects, and amphibians are commonly found in lotic systems. Plants must be able to adapt to the flowing water. Fish and amphibians survive by swimming.

APPLYING WHAT YOU HAVE LEARNED

★ List two ways in which a lentic system and a lotic system differ.

1. _____

2. _____

FORESTS

Forests exist in land areas with enough rainfall to support trees. **Temperate forests** develop in regions with changing seasons: a hot summer, cool fall, cold winter, and a warm spring. Many trees change colors in fall and lose their leaves. There is a wide range of plant and animal life. Organisms in this type of ecosystem must be able to adapt to changing seasons. Some animals move south or **hibernate** *(body functions slow down)* in the winter. **Tropical rainforests** develop in areas where there is ample rainfall and warm temperatures year-round. Large trees cover the forest with their leaves, forming a dense **canopy**. Tropical rain forests have many forms of animal and plant life, with more types of organisms than any other type of ecosystem. They are home to more than half of the world's living plant and animal species.

GRASSLANDS

Grassland areas are found where the climate is drier than a forest but wetter than a desert. There is not enough rainfall to support many trees. Without trees blocking the sunlight, grasses cover the soil. Large grazing animals like cattle, antelope and bison can survive in these regions by eating grass. **Prairies** are grasslands with cold winters and hot summers.

Cattle are found mainly in grassland areas.

DESERTS

Deserts are regions that receive less than 10 inches of rainfall each year. Deserts have their own special forms of plant and animal life. These plants and animals have adapted to the lack of water and extremes of temperature. A **cactus**, for example, stores water in its stem. Its wide, shallow roots catch water from a large surface area. A **camel** can go for long periods without water. Many insects and reptiles have also adapted well to deserts.

TUNDRA

Tundra exists in cold regions, where the soil below the surface stays frozen throughout the year. There are almost no trees, but there are mosses, grasses, fish, birds and even mammals.

HUMAN-MADE ECOSYSTEMS

Some ecosystems exist in human-made environments. For example, farmers may plant a cornfield. The farmer breaks up the soil, plants corn seeds in rows, adds fertilizer to the soil, and gives additional water to the cornplants. The cornplants depend on these activities by the farmer in order to grow. They also depend on the nonliving parts of this ecosystem, such as the sunlight, soil, climate, and water from rainfall. These nonliving parts supply the energy, carbon dioxide gas and water needed for photosynthesis.

Even a city park or playground is a type of ecosystem. Park staff provide seeds, fertilizer, and water to grow grass. They also provide benches and walkways. The grass makes its own food from sunlight, water and carbon dioxide through photosynthesis. Fertilizer adds nutrients to the soil to help the grass grow. People, grass, other plants, and nonliving things interact in this human-made ecosystem.

A city park is a type of ecosystem.

APPLYING WHAT YOU HAVE LEARNED

★ Select **one** of the ecosystems you have just read about.

• For your selection, list some of the plants and animals found there.

_____

_____

• Describe some of the special characteristics that help these plants and animals survive in their environment. _____

_____

_____

ECOSYSTEM INTERACTIONS

The organisms in an ecosystem interact in different ways.

COMPETITION

Competition is the struggle for resources. Similar types of organisms in the same ecosystem will compete for food, water and space. For example, both antelopes and zebras eat grass on the African plains. If there are more zebras, they will eat more grass. Then there is less grass for the antelopes. If there is less grass for the antelopes to eat, their numbers will decrease.

Antelopes and zebras compete for grass.

PREDATORS AND PREY

Many animals live by eating only plants. However, some animals survive by eating other animals. For example, lions on the African grasslands cannot eat and digest grass. They can only survive by eating other animals. An animal that lives by hunting and eating other animals is called a

A linx (predator) chases a rabbit (prey).

predator. The animal that is hunted is known as its **prey**.

Predators have special adaptations to help them hunt better. These characteristics may include speed, the ability to sneak up while approaching prey, and strong senses of smell, sight and hearing.

Prey also have special characteristics to help them survive. Many types of prey have eyes on the sides of their head. This helps them to see if predators are coming from any direction. Horses, antelopes and zebras can run very fast. This helps them to run away when they are in danger of being attacked.

A lion (predator) captures a zebra (prey).

Porcupines have sharp spikes, known as quills, which will hurt a possible predator. When alarmed, a porcupine raises its quills. Some porcupines shake them to produce a rattling sound. If that does not work, the porcupine charges backwards with its quills raised.

Why are sharp quills useful to a porcupine?

COOPERATION

Sometimes there is a cooperative relationship between different plants and animals. In this situation, both the plants and animals benefit. For example, bees collect pollen from the flowers of plants. The bees bring the pollen back to their hive to eat. The plant also benefits. As the bees collect pollen, they pass pollen from one plant to the flowers of other plants. This helps the plants to form seeds.

APPLYING WHAT YOU HAVE LEARNED

★ Think of a predator that you are familiar with. What are some of the special characteristics of this animal that help it to capture prey?

_____

_____

★ Think of another animal that is prey. What special adaptations does this animal have that help it to escape from predators?

_____

THE FLOW OF ENERGY AND NUTRIENTS IN AN ECOSYSTEM

The producers in an ecosystem bring in energy. This same energy then flows through the ecosystem.

PRODUCERS

The plants in the ecosystem are known as **producers** because they make their own food from sunlight, water and carbon dioxide through **photosynthesis.** They change energy from sunlight into chemical energy, which then enters the ecosystem. All the energy in every ecosystem originally comes from this source. The plants also take in **carbon dioxide** from the air and produce **oxygen**. This oxygen can be used by animals.

CONSUMERS

The animals in an ecosystem do not make their own food. They are called **consumers** because they must eat plants or other animals to survive. When a consumer eats a plant or animal, it absorbs some of its energy. Animals also breathe in **oxygen** from the air and produce carbon dioxide. This **carbon dioxide** can be used by plants.

DECOMPOSERS

Some living things in the ecosystem, like worms, fungi, and bacteria, live by breaking down waste products and dead organisms. These are known as **decomposers**. They put **nutrients** back into the soil, which are needed by plants.

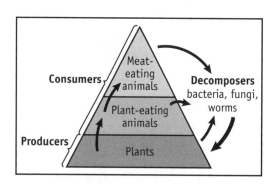

APPLYING WHAT YOU HAVE LEARNED

★ In what ways are producers, consumers, and decomposers different?

_____

_____

APPLYING WHAT YOU HAVE LEARNED

★ Examine the following list of organisms in an ecosystem. Identify each one as a producer, consumer, or decomposer:

Organism	Producer, Consumer, or Decomposer?	Organism	Producer, Consumer, or Decomposer?
Worm		Bacteria	
Deer		Mouse	
Pine Tree		Wheat	
Bear		Algae	
Rabbit		Sparrow	
Fungi		Frog	

FOOD CHAIN

A **food chain** shows how several living things in an ecosystem relate. Here is a food chain showing organisms from the same praire ecosystem:

In this food chain, rabbits eat the grass. Then coyotes eat the rabbits. In this example, the grass stores energy from sunlight (*photosynthesis*). The rabbits take in this energy when they eat grass. Coyotes absorb some of this energy when they eat the rabbits. In this way, a food chain traces the flow of energy in an ecosystem. The direction of the arrows shows how the energy moves. It also shows who eats what.

FOOD WEB

A **food web** shows how several living things in a ecosystem interact together. On the next page is a food web from the same prairie system.

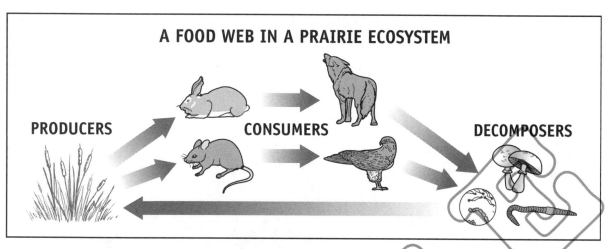

This example shows how nutrients as well as energy are recycled in an ecosystem. When the prairie grasses, rabbits and coyotes die, their bodies decay. Worms, bacteria and other decomposers break down their remains and return chemicals from their bodies to the soil. From the soil, these chemicals are absorbed by the roots of plants. Then the cycle begins all over again.

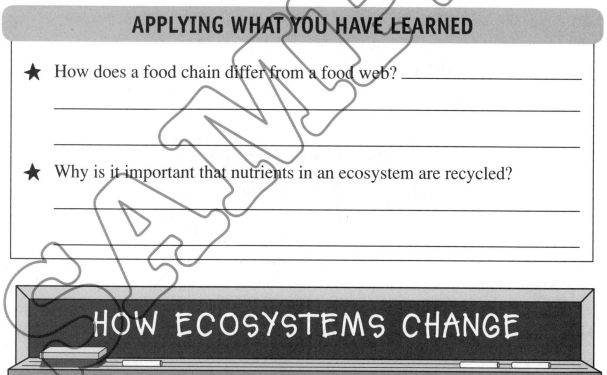

APPLYING WHAT YOU HAVE LEARNED

★ How does a food chain differ from a food web? _____

_____

_____

★ Why is it important that nutrients in an ecosystem are recycled?

_____

_____

HOW ECOSYSTEMS CHANGE

Ecosystems sometimes change. When change occurs in an ecosystem, it can affect all the organisms in the ecosystem. Changes to the habitat or ecosystem in which a plant or animal lives can sometimes be helpful. Very often, however, such changes are harmful to the plants and animals in the ecosystem.

Changes to an ecosystem may make it more difficult for an organism to find food and shelter or to meet any of its other basic needs. An organism may sometimes adapt to the new conditions by changing its behavior. For example, it may start to eat something else. Or the organism may leave the ecosystem and **migrate** to another area. If it cannot adapt to the new conditions or migrate, the organism may die.

When changes to an ecosystem take place slowly, plants and animals have time to adjust to those changes. When changes happen rapidly, some types of plants and animals may not be able to adapt. For example, if the climate of an area gets drier, animals may not have enough to drink. These organisms can no longer meet their basic needs. Those animals may even die out and become **extinct**. Extinction occurs when there is no more of that

Huge herds of mammoths that once roamed the Earth are now extinct.

type of plant or animal left on Earth. Throughout Earth's long history, many organisms have become extinct. These include dinosaurs, saber-tooth tigers, and mammoths.

SEASONAL CHANGE

In many parts of the world, the climate changes during each of the four seasons. In late fall and winter, days become shorter and colder. The nights become longer. In late spring and summer, days grow longer and warmer. In winter, there is less sunlight and less available food. Plants and animals adapt to these changes in various ways. Many plants lose their leaves in winter when less sunlight is available. Some animals, like ground squirrels and bats, **hibernate** (*enter into a deep sleep*) for most of the winter. Since they do not move around, they use much less energy and require less food. Other animals, like birds, fly south to avoid harsh winter weather.

APPLYING WHAT YOU HAVE LEARNED

★ Describe one example of how an organism adjusts to a change in season.

_____

_____

THE DESTRUCTION OF ECOSYSTEMS

Sometimes natural events or human activities can actually destroy an ecosystem. A fire from lightning may burn down a forest. A flood may kill plants and animals on a grassland near a river. Humans may build a dam that floods an area, or a factory may pollute a lake with chemicals.

Although the plants and animals living in a region may be destroyed, new organisms will soon spring up in their place. For example, weeds, grasses and wildflowers will grow in the ashes left by a forest fire. Soon shrubs and short trees will also begin to grow. Later, taller trees will take root. As these trees grow taller, they will block the sunlight. The shorter shrubs will die out. After several hundred years, the area will become a dense forest again.

APPLYING WHAT YOU HAVE LEARNED

★ On a separate sheet of paper, make a series of drawings. Your drawings should show what happens to an area after a severe flood or fire. Show the area at four stages: (**1**) before the flood or fire; (**2**) during the flood or fire; (**3**) ten years after the flood or fire; and (**4**) 100 years later.

THE IMPACT OF HUMAN ACTIVITIES

Humans form a part of the ecosystems where they live. Like other organisms, humans depend on both the nonliving and living environment. For example, many of our everyday activities depend on the natural environment around us. We need water from lakes and reservoirs in order to wash, drink, and cook. Farmers need fertile soil, fresh water and sunlight to grow the crops we eat. Manufacturers need water, raw materials, and energy to make the things we use.

LAND USE

Humans, like other organisms, need land or space in which to live and conduct their activities. Communities use their land in different ways. Some areas are used for housing. Other areas are used for manufacturing or shopping. Still other areas are used for farming. Finally, some areas, like lakes and city parks, are set aside by communities for recreational use, such as swimming, hiking and boating.

FOOD

Humans depend on their natural environment to grow food. Farmers depend on sunshine, rainfall, and soil. Different regions grow different crops because of differences in their physical environment. In Florida, the warm and sunny climate is good for growing oranges. In the Midwest, farmers grow grains like corn and wheat. Western Pennsylvania is good for dairy farming and growing crops like corn.

CLOTHING

Humans depend on the natural environment for the natural **fibers** they need to make most clothes. These fibers can be twisted into thread or yarn. For example, farmers grow cotton or they raise sheep for their wool.

APPLYING WHAT YOU HAVE LEARNED

★ Identify one area near your home and explain how the people there depend on their natural environment. _____

_____

AGRICULTURAL PRODUCTION

Farmers use local ecosystems to encourage the growth of the plants and animals they need. For example, they break up the soil by plowing. Then they plant seeds, add water by irrigation, and add fertilizer to increase the nutrients in the soil. Later, they cut down and collect crops by harvesting. Farmers conduct these activities using special tools and machines, like plows, tractors and harvesters. The food we eat and most of the clothes we wear can be traced back to crops or livestock raised on farms:

CROPS

Grains	Corn, wheat barley
Beans	Soybeans, green beans
Vegetables	Lettuce, squash, cabbage
Fruits	Pears, oranges, lemons

MEATS

Animal	Meat
Pig	Pork, bacon
Cattle (cow)	Beef
Chicken	Chicken

NATURAL FIBERS

Plant	Cloth
Cotton plant	Cotton cloth
Flax	Linen cloth
Wool from sheep	Woolen cloth

FROM FARM LAND TO YOUR KITCHEN TABLE

Farmers plow the soil and plant seeds for wheat. 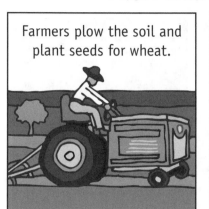	After watering and fertilizing, the seeds grow into fields of wheat. 	Farmers then harvest the wheat by cutting it. 
Farmers separate the wheat grains from the rest of the plant. 	The wheat is then sent to a mill where it is ground into flour. 	The flour is mixed with water and yeast and baked into loaves of bread. 

THREATS POSED BY PESTS

As you know, humans and other animals depend on plants and other animals for food. However, there are large numbers of organisms that also feed on plants and animals. Organisms that cause damage to plants and animals are called **pests**. Pests either compete with other organisms for resources or kill other plants and animals to feed on them. In order to grow food, farmers often have to destroy pests that threaten crops. Here are some well-known pests:

INSECT PESTS

★ **Aphids.** Aphids are tiny insects that live on plant leaves and stems. They suck their juices and weaken crops.

★ **Ticks.** These are small insects that live on the skin and suck the blood of animals.

Deer Tick

OTHER ANIMAL PESTS

★ **Starlings.** These small non-native birds compete with other birds for food.

★ **Zebra Mussels.** These shellfish were recently introduced into the Great Lakes. They spread very quickly and compete for food with local shellfish.

★ **Mice.** These small mammals eat grains and other crops. They compete with humans for resources.

Zebra Mussels

FUNGI

★ **Mold.** These organisms cause food to spoil. Molds can grow on almost any surface when moisture is present.

PLANT PESTS

★ **Foxtail.** This type of grass invades fields.

★ **Purple Loosestrife.** These plants with purple flowers have invaded wetlands once occupied by other plants.

★ **Eurasian Water Milfoil.** These fast-growing plants form thick mats in swamps and lakes. They interfere with recreation.

Loosestrife growing in a swamp.

Humans often use **pesticides** (*chemical poisons*) to kill insects and other pests. However, pesticide use comes with risks. Pesticides can poison the environment.

THREATS TO THE ENVIRONMENT

Many human activities now pose threats to the natural environment. Communities produce wastes — garbage, used packaging materials, cardboard boxes and newspapers, and sewage. This waste can be buried in the ground as **landfill**, **dumped** in the ocean, or **burned**. These solutions add pollution to the land, air or water. Humans create further pollution by burning

A barge about to dump garbage at sea.

fuels like coal and oil. These add carbon dioxide gas to the atmosphere. This gas keeps heat from escaping into space and causes **global warming**, a heating of Earth's average temperatures. Scientists are now trying to find solutions to these problems.

APPLYING WHAT YOU HAVE LEARNED

★ How are wastes dealt with in your community? _____

★ Why is recycling important for the environment? _____

_____

WHAT YOU SHOULD KNOW

☐ You should know that an ecosystem is made up of all living and nonliving things in an area. The living organisms in an ecosystem depend on the living and nonliving parts of the ecosystem to survive.

☐ You should know that energy and nutrients are cycled through an ecosystem. Plants trap energy from the sun. Animals eat plants and other animals. Similar organisms in an ecosystem compete with each other for resources, such as oxygen, water, food or space.

☐ You should know that changes in the environment can cause changes in an ecosystem. Human activities affect the environment.

LESSON STUDY CARDS

Ecosystems

Ecosystem. All the living and nonliving things interacting in an area.

★ **Adaptations.** The characteristics of a plant or animal that help it survive and reproduce in its environment.

★ **Competition.** Plants and animals often compete with each other for the same resources.

★ Organisms in an ecosystem depend on both its living and nonliving parts.

Flow of Energy in an Ecosystem

★ **Producers.** Plants produce their own food.

★ **Consumers.** Animals eat plants or animals for energy. **Predators** are animals that hunt and kill **prey.**

★ **Decomposers.** Worms, bacteria, and fungi break down wastes and dead plants and animals; they return nutrients to the soil.

★ **Food Chain/Food Web.** These are diagrams that show how energy flows through an ecosystem; who eats what.

Examples of Ecosystems

★ **Lentic Systems**   ★ **Deserts**
★ **Lotic Systems**   ★ **Tundra**
★ **Forests**

Changes in Ecosystems

★ Plants and animals may adapt to seasonal changes: plants lose leaves; some animals migrate or **hibernate**.

★ Some organisms cannot adapt to rapid changes and become **extinct** (*die out*).

★ Floods, fires, humans can destroy ecosystems; the area then undergoes a series of changes.

Impact of Human Activities

★ Humans depend on the environment for food, clothing, and recreation.

★ Food comes from farming grains, fruits, vegetables and beans, and from raising livestock, such as cattle, pigs, and chickens.

★ Clothing often comes from natural fibers such as cotton, flax (*linen*) and wool (*sheep*).

★ Human activities threaten the environment by causing water and air pollution and by the dumping of waste in the environment.

CHECKING YOUR UNDERSTANDING

Use the diagram below to answer question 1.

1. Which correctly shows a food chain in this ecosystem?

   A   grass ➜ cow ➜ human
   B   cow ➜ grass ➜ human
   C   tree ➜ bird ➜ caterpillar
   D   caterpillar ➜ tree ➜ human

   S4.B
   3.1.2

> **HINT**
> *To answer this question correctly, you must recall that a food chain shows the flow of energy in an ecosystem. Food is created by plants using the energy of the sun (photosynthesis). These plants are eaten by animals. Other larger and faster animals may eat these animals. In this case, the food chain starts with the grass. Cows eat the grass. Humans eat beef from the cows. The correct answer is **Choice A**.*

Now answer some other questions on your own. Circle the correct answer.

2. Antelopes eat grass on the plains of Africa. Antelopes are the prey of lions and other predators. Which specific adaptation is most helpful to antelopes?

    A   brightly colored fur
    B   sharp claws
    C   fast, strong legs
    D   small eyes

> ◆ **Examine the Question**
> ◆ **Recall What You Know**
> ◆ **Apply What You Know**

S4.B 2.1.2

3. How do decomposers help the parts of an ecosystem keep in balance?

    A   They return nutrients to the soil.
    B   They eat producers.
    C   They make food through photosynthesis.
    D   They provide food for consumers.

S4.B 3.1.2

4. How do plants in streams differ from plants in ponds?

    A   They can live underwater.
    B   They can survive the fast flow of water.
    C   They need sunlight to produce food.
    D   They are threatened by the Eurasian water milfoil.

S4.B 3.1.1

5. Bats spend each winter in a deep sleep. Which statement **best** describes how these types of bats adapt to seasonal changes in their ecosystem?

    A   They migrate to warmer areas.
    B   They hibernate in winter.
    C   They hunt for longer periods in summer.
    D   They drink less water during summer months.

S4.B 3.2.3

6. How are humans dependent on plants and animals for their clothing?

    A   Most food can be traced back to plants.
    B   Humans can eat both plants and other animals.
    C   Animals provide energy needed to run machines.
    D   Plants and animals provide natural fibers.

S4.B 3.3.2

Use the diagram below to answer question 7.

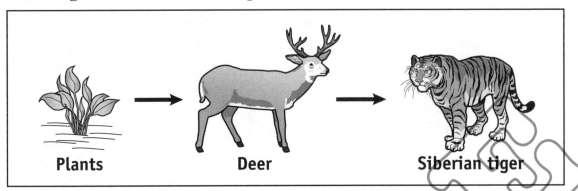

Plants　　　　**Deer**　　　　**Siberian tiger**

7.　What would be the best title for this diagram?

   A　Plant and animal differences

   B　Animals that are threatened

   C　All the living things in an ecosystem

   D　Energy flow in an ecosystem

♦ Examine the Question
♦ Recall What You Know
♦ Apply What You Know

S4.B
3.1.2

8.　Which statement **best** identifies aphids?

   A　They are used to fertilize different farm crops.

   B　Humans depend on them to kill off starling birds.

   C　They live on plant leaves and stems and can kill crops.

   D　They help farmers kill insects that threaten crops.

S4.B
3.3.3

9.　The flow of energy through an ecosystem is important to the survival of plants and animals in that ecosystem.

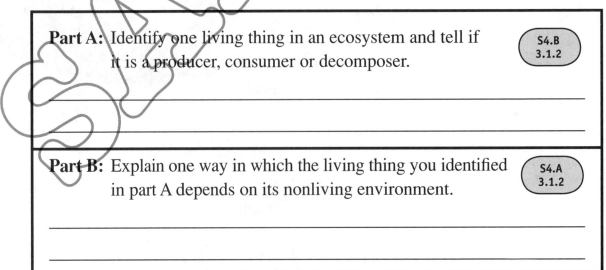

Part A: Identify one living thing in an ecosystem and tell if it is a producer, consumer or decomposer.

S4.B
3.1.2

Part B: Explain one way in which the living thing you identified in part A depends on its nonliving environment.

S4.A
3.1.2

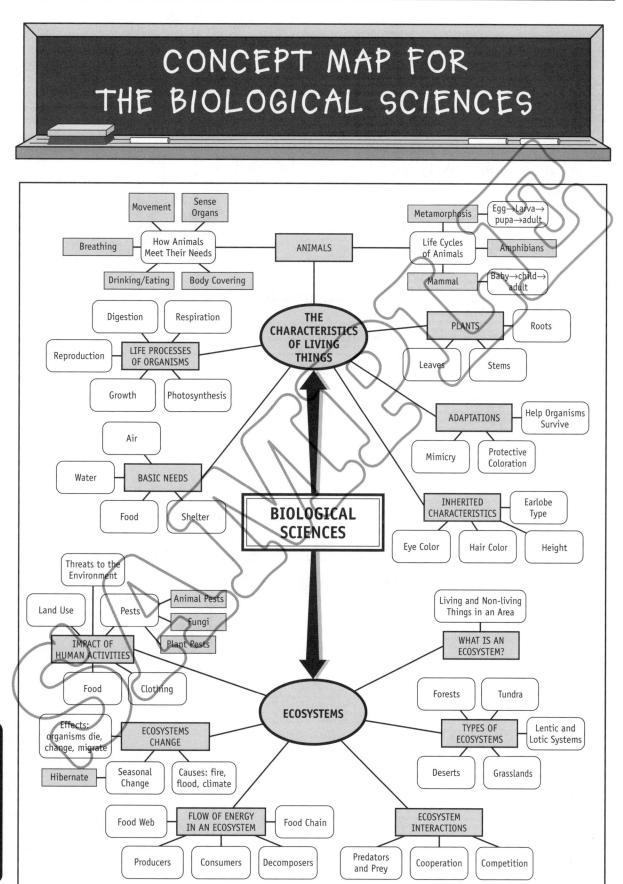

TESTING YOUR UNDERSTANDING

1. A fire caused by lightning destroyed this forest. What will **most likely** happen to the birds that lived in this forest?

   A   They will change the type of shelter they use.
   B   They will fly to another forest or die.
   C   They will change the foods they eat.
   D   They will adapt by living on the ground.

   S4.A
   1.3.4

Use the diagram below to answer question 2.

FOOD CHAIN

2. Which would **best** complete this food chain?

   A   lemons   B   insects
   C   tigers   D   owls

   S4.B
   3.1.2

3. Many plants produce seeds. Often these seeds are spread by the wind. Which seed type is **most likely** to be spread by the wind?

   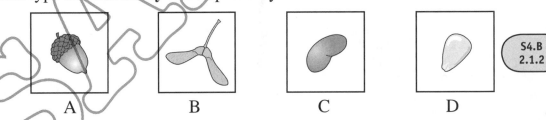

   A   B   C   D

   S4.B
   2.1.2

4. What basic need do birds meet by returning to their nests in trees with worms they have captured?

   A   water
   S4.B
   1.1.3
   B   food
   C   shelter
   D   air

5. Which statement **best** explains why animals are unable to survive in a closed terrarium without plants?

A   Plants produce the oxygen and food that animals need.

B   Animals need carbon dioxide to survive.

C   Plants give off water which animals need to survive.

D   Plants are unable to move, while animals move freely.

S4.B
3.1.2

6. Which of these can be identified as a producer?

A   B   C   D

S4.B
3.1.2

7. Anteaters live in tropical forests. They survive by eating ants. Anteaters hunt ants by sticking their long snouts and tongues in the ground where ants live. Which statement **best** explains how the anteater's long snout and tongue help it to survive in its environment?

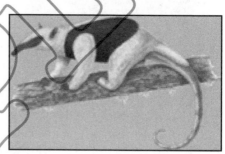

A   It helps it to hide in trees.

B   It helps it to catch water.

C   It helps it to find ants.

D   It helps it to escape predators.

S4.B
2.1.2

8. How are molds and ticks similar?

A   They prevent starlings from eating fruits.

B   They live on the skin of animals.

C   They can both be pests.

D   They help farmers to destroy insects.

S4.B
3.3.3

9. How does the stinger on a wasp help it to survive?

A   It attracts other wasps.

S4.B
2.1.2

B   It is used to carry food.

C   It allows a wasp to build its home.

D   It protects the wasp from its enemies.

Stinger and a droplet of wasp venom.

10. Which characteristic has influenced the type of plants living in the environment shown to the right?

S4.B 2.1.1

A   lack of sunlight

B   too little rainfall for many trees

C   extreme cold throughout the year

D   frequent floods from heavy rains

Use the pictures below to answer question 11.

A Turtle

A Hippopotamus

11. What external characteristic do turtles and hippopotamuses have in common?

S4.A 1.1.2

A   They have long necks to see enemies from a distance.

B   They can move quickly to escape predators.

C   They have thick body coverings that make them hard to eat.

D   They have sharp teeth to attack their prey.

12. Which picture shows the correct order of steps in the life cycle of a plant?

S4.B 1.1.5

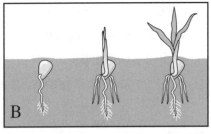

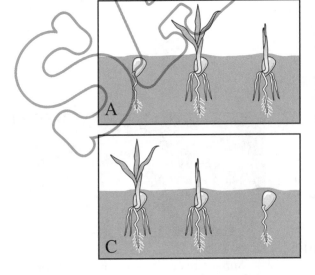

13. Plants have several basic needs that they must meet to survive.

> **Part A:** Identify one basic need of every plant.   (S4.B 1.1.3)
>
> _____
>
> **Part B:** Explain how the different parts of a plant work together (S4.B 1.1.4) to meet the need you identified in your answer to part A.
>
> _____
>
> _____

CHECKLIST OF ELIGIBLE CONTENT

☐ **S4.A.1.3.4** You should be able to explain what happens to a living organism when its food supply, access to water, shelter, or space is changed (e.g., it might die, migrate, change behavior, eat something else). [**Lesson 10**]

☐ **S4.A.1.3.5** You should be able to provide examples, predict or describe how everyday human activities (e.g., solid waste production, food production and consumption, transportation, water consumption, energy production and use) may change the environment. [**Lesson 10**]

☐ **S4.A.3.1.2** You should be able to explain a relationship between the living and nonliving components in a system (e.g., food web, terrarium). [**Lesson 10**]

☐ **S4.A.3.1.3** You should be able to categorize the parts of an ecosystem as either living or nonliving and describe their roles in the system. [**Lesson 10**]

☐ **S4.A.3.1.4** You should be able to identify the parts of the food and fiber systems as they relate to agricultural products from the source to the consumer. [**Lesson 10**]

☐ **S4.A.3.3.1** You should be able to identify and describe observable patterns (e.g., growth patterns in plants, weather, water cycle). [**Lesson 10**]

☐ **S4.B.1.1.1** You should be able to identify life processes of living things (e.g., growth, digestion, respiration). [**Lesson 9**]

☐ **S4.B.1.1.2** You should be able to compare similar functions of external characteristics of organisms (e.g., anatomical characteristics: appendages, type of covering, body segments). [**Lesson 9**]

☐ **S4.B.1.1.3** You should be able to describe basic needs of plants and animals (e.g., air, water, food). [**Lesson 9**]

☐ **S4.B.1.1.4** You should be able to describe how different parts of a living thing work together to provide what the organism needs (e.g., parts of plants: roots, stems, leaves). **[Lesson 9]**

☐ **S4.B.1.1.5** You should be able to describe the life cycles of different organisms (e.g., moth, grasshopper, frog, seed-producing plant). **[Lesson 9]**

☐ **S4.B.2.1.1** You should be able to identify characteristics for plant and animal survival in different environments (e.g., wetland, tundra, desert, prairie, deep ocean, forest). **[Lesson 9]**

☐ **S4.B.2.1.2** You should be able to explain how specific adaptations can help a living organism survive (e.g., protective coloration, mimicry, leaf sizes and shapes, ability to catch or retain water). **[Lesson 9]**

☐ **S4.B.2.2.1** You should be able to identify physical characteristics (e.g., height, hair color, eye color, attached earlobes, ability to roll tongue) that appear in both parents and could be passed on to offspring. **[Lesson 9]**

☐ **S4.B.3.1.1** You should be able to describe the living and nonliving components of a local ecosystem (e.g., lentic and lotic systems, forest, cornfield, grasslands, city park, playground). **[Lesson 10]**

☐ **S4.B.3.1.2** You should be able to describe interactions between living and nonliving components (e.g., plants — water, soil, sunlight, carbon dioxide, temperature; animals — food, water, shelter, oxygen, temperature) of a local ecosystem. **[Lesson 10]**

☐ **S4.B.3.2.1** You should be able to describe what happens to a living thing when its habitat is changed. **[Lesson 10]**

☐ **S4.B.3.2.2** You should be able to describe and predict how changes in the environment (e.g., fire, pollution, floods) can affect systems. **[Lesson 10]**

☐ **S4.B.3.2.3** You should be able to explain and predict how changes in seasons affect plants, animals, or daily human life (e.g., food availability, shelter, mobility). **[Lesson 10]**

☐ **S4.B.3.3.1** You should be able to identify everyday human activities (e.g., driving, washing, eating, manufacturing, farming) within a community that depend on the natural environment. **[Lesson 10]**

☐ **S4.B.3.3.2** You should be able to describe the human dependence on the food and fiber systems from production to consumption (e.g., food, clothing, shelter, products). **[Lesson 10]**

☐ **S4.B.3.3.3** You should be able to identify biological pests (e.g., fungi – molds, plants — foxtail, purple loosestrife, Eurasian water milfoil; animals — aphids, ticks, zebra mussels, starlings, mice) that compete with humans for resources. **[Lesson 10]**

☐ **S4.B.3.3.4** You should be able to identify major land uses in the urban, suburban and rural communities (e.g., housing, commercial, recreation). **[Lesson 10]**

☐ **S4.B.3.3.5** You should be able to describe the effects of pollution (e.g., litter) in the community. **[Lesson 10]**

☐ **S4.D.1.3.3** You should be able to describe or compare lentic systems (i.e. ponds, lakes, and bays) and lotic systems (i.e., streams, creeks and rivers). **[Lesson 10]**

UNIT 4　PHYSICAL SCIENCES

In this unit, you will learn about the physical sciences. The **physical sciences** study matter, motion and energy.

Matter makes up all the objects around you. It includes anything that takes up space and has mass.

If matter can be thought of as all objects around you, **energy** is what **moves** matter. In this unit, you will learn that energy has the ability to move or change matter. Electricity, heat, light, and sound are all different forms of energy.

★ **Lesson 11: The Properties of Matter.** In this lesson, you will learn about matter and its observable properties, such as mass and conductivity. You will also learn how matter can change its form from solid to liquid to gas. Finally, you will learn to classify objects based on their properties.

★ **Lesson 12: Motion, Force, and Energy.** In this lesson, you will learn how matter moves and how force is needed for matter to move or change. You will also learn how energy provides this force. There are many types of energy, and one type of energy can change into another.

KEY TERMS YOU WILL LEARN ABOUT IN THIS UNIT

- Matter
- Physical Properties
- States of Matter
- Solid, Liquid, Gas
- Mass, Volume

- Energy
- Magnetism
- Conductivity
- Position
- Motion

- Force
- Gravity
- Friction
- Series Circuit
- Parallel Circuit

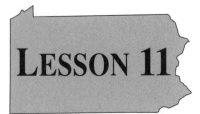

LESSON 11

THE PROPERTIES OF MATTER

In this chapter, you will learn about the properties of matter.

— IMPORTANT IDEAS —

A. Each piece of **matter** can be described by its physical properties.

B. The physical properties of matter include mass, shape, volume, color, texture, magnetism, state and conductivity.

C. Matter has three **states**: solid, liquid, or gas.

D. Objects can be **classified** or grouped based on their physical characteristics.

WHAT IS MATTER?

What do a strawberry, chocolate cake and air have in common? If you said they were different types of **matter**, you would be correct.

Matter is everything that takes up space (*volume*) and has mass. Matter comes in different shapes and sizes. For example, air and water are both forms of matter. This book is matter. A diamond ring, sand on a beach, and clouds in the sky are all different forms of matter. However, **NOT EVERYTHING** is matter. Light and electricity are not matter. They do not have mass and they do not take up their own separate space.

APPLYING WHAT YOU HAVE LEARNED

Identify two examples of matter and two things that are not matter.

MATTER	NOT MATTER
1. _____	1. _____
2. _____	2. _____

THE PROPERTIES OF MATTER

Every piece of matter has certain **properties**. A **property** is any characteristic or quality that something has. Scientists use different ways to describe matter. Some properties they use to describe matter include:

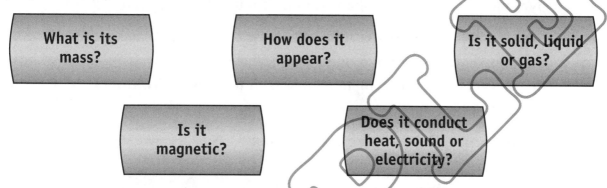

What is its mass?

How does it appear?

Is it solid, liquid or gas?

Is it magnetic?

Does it conduct heat, sound or electricity?

Scientists are able to use these observable physical properties to describe and classify different kinds of matter. Let's look at each of these properties more closely.

MASS AND WEIGHT

As you already know, **mass** is *how much* there is of an object — the *amount* of matter in an object. Scientists usually measure mass in **grams** (g) or **kilograms** (kg). You might recall that scientists use a **double-pan** or **triple-beam** balance to measure mass.

Although mass and weight are related, they are different. On Earth, an object's **weight** is the force of attraction created by **gravity**. Our weight would change if we went to the moon or another planet. The chart below shows what a student who weighed 80 pounds on Earth would weigh on Mars and the moon. However, his **mass** *stays the same*.

A Person's Mass	Earth Weight	Mars Weight	Moon Weight
	80 pounds*	30 pounds*	13 pounds*

*Pounds can be used either as units of mass or of weight.

APPEARANCE AND SIZE

Every piece of matter has its own appearance and size.

★ **Color, Texture, Shape.** Every piece of matter, for example, has some color. It also has some **texture** (*how it feels*) — such as hard, soft, rough, or smooth. **Metals**, for example, are usually hard, smooth, and shiny. Finally, each piece of matter has its own **shape**. For example, it might be a sphere, pyramid or cube. Or the shape might be curved or irregular.

★ **Size.** Each piece of matter also has its own size — how large or small it is. Size can be measured in length, width, mass or volume. You already know that **mass** is how much matter there is in the object. **Volume** is how much space the object takes up.

★ **Relative Size.** Relative size concerns how large one piece of matter is compared to another. One object may have much more matter than another. It will be heavier. It may also take up more space. For example, a bowling ball has more volume as well as more mass than a baseball. Thus, its **relative size** is greater.

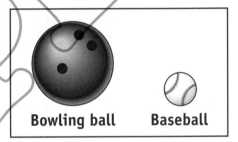

Bowling ball   Baseball

THE THREE STATES OF MATTER

Each type of matter can exist in three **states**, or forms — as a **solid**, **liquid** or **gas**. You might think of iron as a solid. However, when iron is heated to a very high temperature it melts. You may think of water as a liquid, but if it cools down enough, it becomes a solid. The reason for these different states is that all matter is actually made up of tiny particles. These

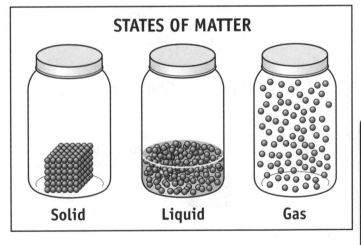

STATES OF MATTER

Solid   Liquid   Gas

particles are so small we cannot see them. These particles are constantly moving.

SOLIDS

In a **solid**, these tiny particles are locked into fixed positions. As a result, they give the substance a **fixed volume** and **shape**. The particles of a solid are moving, but they vibrate in place. A rock and an ice cube are both solids.

LIQUIDS

When heat is applied to a solid, its particles begin to vibrate faster. Eventually, its particles vibrate so much that they start to move around each other. The solid melts and becomes a **liquid**. Some examples of liquids at room temperature are water and milk. Since the particles of a liquid can move around each other, a liquid can change its shape easily. A liquid will take the shape of whatever container it is in. For example, if you pour some milk from a milk carton into a glass, the milk will take the shape of the glass it fills. Its volume, however, stays the same.

GASES

If heat is applied to a liquid, its particles move around even faster. Eventually, its tiny particles move so rapidly that they spread out in all directions as a **gas**. A gas has no fixed shape or fixed volume. It fills up whatever space it has. Some examples of common gases are oxygen and carbon dioxide.

APPLYING WHAT YOU HAVE LEARNED

★ Explain how solids, liquids and gases differ from each other. Complete the chart by filling in the blank items. Then draw a picture illustrating each.

Characteristic	Solid	Liquid	Gas
Shape			No fixed shape
Volume		Has a fixed volume	
Your Picture			

APPLYING WHAT YOU HAVE LEARNED

★ Describe what will happen to the water in each beaker.

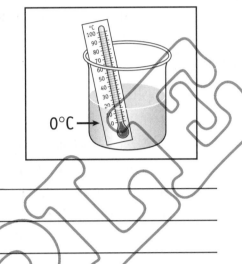

MAGNETISM

A **magnet** is a piece of metal that attracts some other metals, such as **iron**, **nickel**, and **steel**. A magnet pulls pieces of those metals towards it. It can even pick some of them up. However, many types of metals are not attracted to magnets. For example, a magnet will have no effect on tin, aluminum, copper, gold or silver. A magnet also has no effect on nonmetals, like plastic, rubber or wood. Scientists sometimes use magnetism to separate magnetic objects from non-magnetic ones.

Iron   Nickel   Steel

APPLYING WHAT YOU HAVE LEARNED

★ A small sliver of iron accidently flew into a child's eye. How might doctors use their knowledge of magnetism to help the child?

APPLYING WHAT YOU HAVE LEARNED

★ Conduct your own experiment at home to see which objects are attracted to magnets. Place each of the following objects next to a magnet to see if it moves. Record your results by placing a check mark (✔) next to those items that are magnetic.

☐ A copper penny   ☐ A steel toy car   ☐ Aluminum foil

☐ A plastic hanger   ☐ An iron nail   ☐ A rubber band

CONDUCTIVITY

Another important property of matter is how well it carries heat, sound or electricity. This ability is known as **conductivity**.

HEAT

Some materials conduct heat better than others. In objects made from these materials, heat moves faster from one end of the object to the other. For example, **metals** like copper and aluminum conduct heat very well. Wood, plastic and rubber do not conduct heat very well. For this reason, wood, plastic and rubber are often used for the handle of a pot. They will not heat up quickly.

SOUND

Sound can travel through liquids and solids as well as through the air. Some materials conduct sound better than others. For example, metal and wood conduct sound better than rubber does.

APPLYING WHAT YOU HAVE LEARNED

Try this experiment at home. Put your ear against a long piece of wood. Ask a parent or friend to tap on the other side of the wood. Now cover that end of the wood with a kitchen sponge. Have your parent or friend tap on it again.

★ Which time was the tapping louder? _____ What might explain this?

_____

_____

APPLYING WHAT YOU HAVE LEARNED

Try this experiment with other materials around your house. Which materials best conduct sound? **(1)** _____

(2) _____   **(3)** _____

ELECTRICITY

Some forms of matter are good conductors of electricity. Metals conduct electricity well. Other materials, like rubber and plastic, cannot conduct electricity. Wires are usually made of copper or some other metal that is a good conductor of electricity. However, the wire will usually be covered in plastic

Copper wire   Insulation

Electricity runs through only the copper wire

or some other material that does not conduct electricity well. In the picture above, the copper at center of the wire is a good conductor of electricity. The copper is covered with a plastic coating that does not conduct electricity. Someone who touches the wire will be protected against a shock from the electricity running through it.

APPLYING WHAT YOU HAVE LEARNED

★ Look around your classroom. Identify four objects that you think are good conductors of heat, electricity or sound.

• _____   • _____

• _____   • _____

CLASSIFYING OBJECTS

Scientists are able to **classify** objects into different groups based on their physical properties or other characteristics.

For example, look at the group of objects listed to the right. All four of these objects are red. They share the physical characteristic of having the same color. For this reason, these objects have all been placed in the same group.

	Red Objects
○	
	• red fire engine
	• stop sign
	• red brick
○	• red balloon

APPLYING WHAT YOU HAVE LEARNED

★ Scientists divided eight objects into four separate pairs. Can you tell what characteristic each pair of items has in common?

Pair of objects	What they have in common
water boiling / hot metal	
ball of cotton / feather pillow	
water / glass window	
copper wire / light bulb	

Notice that both objects in the first pair are very hot. They share the same temperature. Each of the second pair of objects is very soft. The third pair has clear objects. You can see right through both a glass of water and a glass window. The objects in the last pair are both excellent conductors of electricity. As you can see, the two members of each pair above have an important property in common.

Let's see how well you can classify objects based on their properties. First, study the pictures below. They show different objects and some of their observable properties.

| yellow pear | white scarf | gold ring | glass of apple juice |
| glass of milk | brass key | yellow banana | white sweater |

How many ways can you classify these eight objects? Fill in the boxes below according to the characteristic shown. Then compare your list with those of other students in your class.

COLOR	
Yellow/Gold	White
1. _____	1. _____
2. _____	2. _____
3. _____	3. _____
4. _____	
5. _____	

USE	
Food	Not Food
1. _____	1. _____
2. _____	2. _____
3. _____	3. _____
4. _____	4. _____

STATE	
Liquid	Solid
1. _____	1. _____
2. _____	2. _____
	3. _____
	4. _____
	5. _____
	6. _____

As you can see, the same objects can often be classified in different ways. Now let's take a look at some new groups of objects. Several students were asked to classify eight objects into three groups. This is what they did:

Group 1

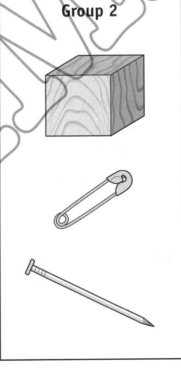

Group 2

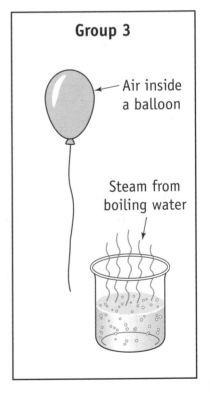

Group 3

Air inside a balloon

Steam from boiling water

APPLYING WHAT YOU HAVE LEARNED

Can you guess which physical property the students used to classify these objects into three groups?

★ Are they classified based on shape? ☐ **Yes** ☐ **No**

Explain your answer. _____

_____

★ Are they classified based on texture? ☐ **Yes** ☐ **No**

Explain your answer. _____

_____

★ Are they classified based on color? ☐ **Yes** ☐ **No**

Explain your answer. _____

_____

★ Are they classified into metals and non-metals? ☐ **Yes** ☐ **No**

Explain your answer. _____

_____

★ Are they classified based on size? ☐ **Yes** ☐ **No**

Explain your answer. _____

_____

★ Are they classified based on state (solid, liquid and gas)? ☐ **Yes** ☐ **No**

Explain your answer. _____

_____

★ What other properties could have been used to regroup these same objects?

(1) _____ (2) _____

WHAT YOU SHOULD KNOW

☐ You should know that matter can be described by its physical properties. These properties include color, shape, volume, mass, texture, magnetism, state and conductivity.

☐ You should know that matter has three states: solid, liquid, and gas.

☐ You should know that objects can be classified or grouped based on their physical properties or other characteristics.

LESSON STUDY CARDS

Properties of Matter

Every type of matter has certain observable physical **properties**.

★ **Mass.** How much there is of an object — the amount of matter measured in grams (g) and kilograms (kg).
★ **Volume.** The space the matter takes up.
★ **State.** If it is a solid, liquid, or gas.
★ **Appearance.** Color, shape and texture.
★ **Magnetism.** Whether or not it is attracted to a magnet.
★ **Conductivity.** How well it carries heat, sound, or electricity.

States of Matter

Matter can exist in one of three forms or states:

★ **Solid.** It has a fixed volume and shape.
★ **Liquid.** It takes the shape of whatever container it is in; its volume stays fixed.
★ **Gas.** Its particles move in all directions. It has no shape and no fixed volume.

Classifying Objects

Objects can be classified or grouped based on their physical or other properties — color, size, texture, shape, conductivity, magnetism, etc.

CHECKING YOUR UNDERSTANDING

1. The students in a science class are given a list of objects to classify. Which physical property could **best** be used to classify these objects into three groups?

    A shape
    C color
    B magnetism
    D state of matter

    S4.C
    1.1.2

○	List of Objects
	• a beaker of milk
	• a yellow pencil
	• a blue car
○	• a waterfall
	• steam from boiling pot of water

HINT *To answer this question, you must understand how physical properties can be used to group objects. Use the physical property in each answer to see how many groups it would create. Choice A would create 5 groups, since each object has its own shape. B would also create 4 groups, since each object has its own color. C would create two groups, because some parts of a car are magnetic while others are not. The best answer is* **Choice D**. *There are three states of matter. One or more objects can be placed in each group — solid: pencil, car; liquid: milk, waterfall; gas: steam.*

Now answer some other questions on your own. Circle the correct answer.

2. Which of the jars below contains a solid?

S4.C
1.1.1

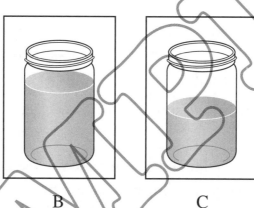

    A   B   C   D

3. Which of the following objects would be attracted to a magnet?

    A   paper bag   B   copper penny   S4.C
    C   rubber ball   D   iron nail   1.1.1

4. A student fills an ice cube tray with water and puts it into the freezer. What happens when water in the ice cube tray freezes?

    A   The liquid becomes a gas.
    B   The gas becomes a liquid.
    C   The liquid becomes a solid.
    D   The solid becomes a liquid.

> ◆ **Examine the Question**
> ◆ **Recall What You Know**
> ◆ **Apply What You Know**

S4.C
1.1.1

5. Which of these objects would be the best conductor of heat?

    A   a rubber glove   B   a copper pot   S4.C
    C   a plastic spoon   D   a wooden handle   1.1.1

Use the pictures below to answer question 6.

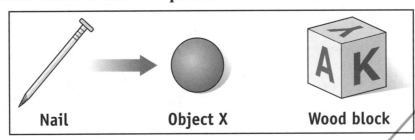

Nail   Object X   Wood block

6. The nail is pulled by Object X, but the wood block next to it does not move. What property does Object X have that attracts the nail?

   A color   B magnetism

   C weight   D mass

   S4.C
   1.1.1

A teacher divided objects into two groups and placed each group in a separate box. Then the teacher asked students to identify how objects in the boxes were grouped.

7. Which response correctly describes how the objects are grouped?

   S4.C
   1.1.2

   A objects that are metal and those that are not metal
   B objects that are large and objects that are tiny
   C objects that are soft and objects that are hard
   D objects that have ridges and those that are sharp

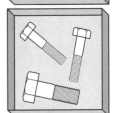

8. Which statement describes a physical property of a candy bar?

   A It is solid.
   B It is usually red in color.
   C It is always large in size.
   D It is an excellent conductor of heat.

   S4.C
   1.1.1

9. What does a student learn when she measures the mass of her soccer ball?

   A How fast it is moving.
   B How much heat it creates.
   C How much matter it contains.
   D How much space it takes up.

   ◆ Examine the Question
   ◆ Recall What You Know
   ◆ Apply What You Know

   S4.C
   1.1.1

10. Which of the following objects would be attracted to a magnet?

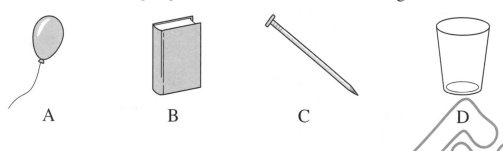

A	B	C	D

Use the diagram below to answer question 11.

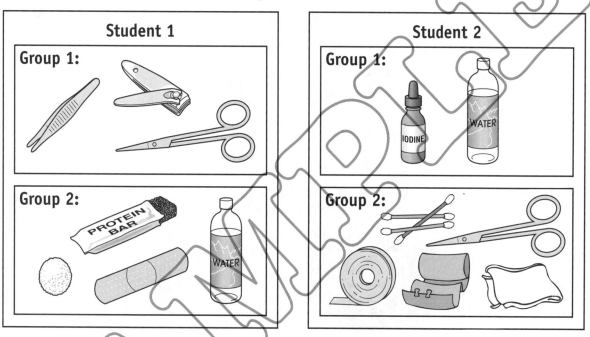

11. A teacher brought a first aid kit to class. Two students created different groups of objects based on their physical properties. Which pair correctly describes how the students grouped the objects?

A   Student 1: objects that taste good and those that do not
    Student 2: objects that are liquids and those that are gases

B   Student 1: objects that are yellow and those that are not
    Student 2: objects that are soft and objects that are hard

C   Student 1: objects that are metals and objects that are not
    Student 2: objects that are liquid and objects that are solids

D   Student 1: objects that can be eaten and those that cannot
    Student 2: objects that are round and objects that are not

S4.C
1.1.2

12. The picture to the right shows a wooden pencil with four parts. Which part of the pencil would be the best conductor of electricity?

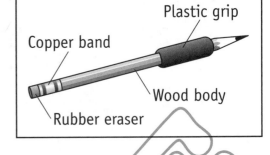

A   its wood body

B   its plastic grip

C   its rubber eraser

D   its copper band

S4.C 1.1.1

13. Which of these jars has the greatest mass?

S4.C 1.1.1

A   B   C   D

Use the diagram below to answer question 14.

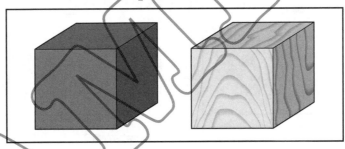

14. The picture above shows two cubes of the same size. The first cube is made of iron. The second cube is made of wood. These two cubes can be compared by looking at their physical properties.

Part A: Name one physical property that can be used to compare these cubes.

S4.C 1.1.1

_____

Part B: For the physical property identified in part A, describe how you would measure that property.

S4.A 2.2.1

_____

_____

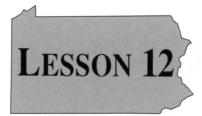

LESSON 12

MOTION, FORCE AND ENERGY

Energy has the ability to **move** matter. In this chapter, you will learn about motion, force, and energy, and how they are related.

— IMPORTANT IDEAS —

A. **Position** is where an object is located compared to other objects. **Motion** is a change in position. Motion can be in a straight line, back and forth, in a circle, or in any other direction.

B. When **force** is applied to an object, it changes its motion. There are many kinds of forces, such as **magnetic force**, **pushes and pulls**, **gravity** and **friction**.

C. **Energy** is an ability to do work. Energy has the power to change or move matter. There are many forms of energy. These include heat, light, electricity, and sound energy. Energy also has the ability to change from one form to another.

D. **Electricity** flows in a circuit. There are **series** and **parallel** circuits.

E. A vibrating object produces sound. Every sound has characteristics such as **loudness** and **pitch**.

MOTION AND FORCE

In the last lesson, you studied matter. In this chapter, you will study what makes matter move and change. Let's begin with position.

Position is the location of an object in relation to other things. For example, you can indicate the position of your pencil based on its distance from the edges of the desk. Your pencil might be one foot from the right side of your desk and one foot from the back edge of your desk.

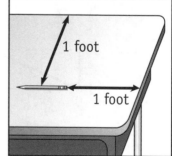

APPLYING WHAT YOU HAVE LEARNED

★ Describe your position now by locating yourself relative to another person or object. _____

_____

Motion occurs when an object changes its position. It goes from one location to another. The length it travels is known as **distance**.

Speed is how **fast** an object is moving. It is the distance an object travels in a specific amount of time. For example, a car may travel 50 miles an hour. This means that every hour, the car travels 50 miles. How many miles would that car travel in two hours? In three hours? Fill in the chart on the right with your answers.

Time	Distance Traveled
1 hour	★ 50 miles
2 hours	★ _____
3 hours	★ _____
4 hours	★ _____
5 hours	★ _____

You can turn this same information into a line graph. Complete the graph below with the information you indicated in the chart:

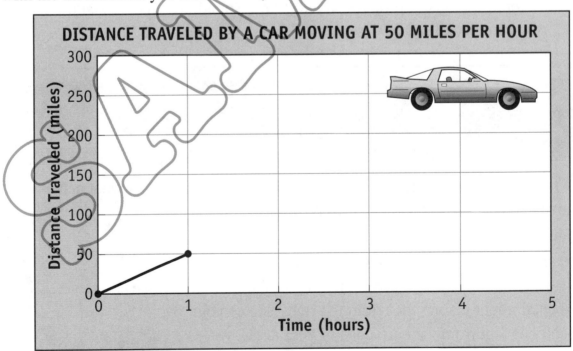

Motion has both speed and direction. **Direction** is where something is moving. An object can move in different directions. For example, a basketball may bounce on the floor. It falls down, bounces up, falls again, and bounces back up again. An arrow may fly ahead in almost a straight line. Some objects move in a circular or curved direction. For example, the moon circles Earth, while Earth moves in a giant circle around the sun.

FORCE CHANGES MOTION

What makes an object move? Have you ever kicked a soccer ball resting on the ground? When you kick a soccer ball, you provide the **force** that makes the ball start to move. The ball flies up and comes down rolling. At some point it will slow down and stop. The ball stops rolling because of **friction**, the rubbing of the ball against the ground. If there were no friction to slow down the ball, it would keep rolling forever — or until some other force stopped it.

A foot applies force to a soccer ball.

All changes in motion are caused by a force of some kind. To start an object moving, whether a soccer ball or car, requires some force. Once moving, an object keeps moving at the same speed and direction until some new force changes or stops it.

In outer space, there is no friction. Moving objects just keep moving at the same speed and direction until they come into contact with some other force. Some outside force is needed to cause each object to slow down, speed up, or change its direction.

APPLYING WHAT YOU HAVE LEARNED

★ What will happen to a rocket ship moving in outer space at 100 km per second if no other force is applied to it?

_____

_____

TYPES OF FORCES

There are many different kinds of forces.

MAGNETIC FORCE

You have already studied magnetism. Magnetism is a type of force. It pulls metal objects towards a magnet.

GRAVITY

You also know about gravity. Earth attracts all objects to its center with this force. The pull of gravity gives objects their weight. Scientists have learned that gravity is a force of attraction between any two objects. Gravity pulls the moon towards Earth, and Earth towards the sun. Gravity increases with the mass of the objects. The force of gravity decreases as two objects move farther apart.

PUSH-AND-PULL FORCES

Sometimes a moving object pushes or pulls at another object. Some motion from the first object will transfer to the second object.

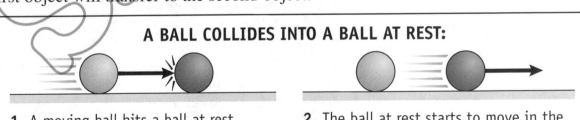

A BALL COLLIDES INTO A BALL AT REST:

1. A moving ball hits a ball at rest.

2. The ball at rest starts to move in the same direction as the moving ball.

FRICTION

Friction is a fourth kind of force. It is the force created when two things rub against each other. As the two objects rub, they grind and drag against each other. This rubbing and grinding slows down their movement against each other. For example, if you rub your two hands together, you create friction. This friction even creates some heat. Your hands will feel warmer.

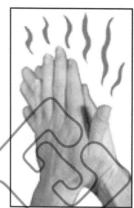

On Earth, moving objects face friction from both the air and ground. The force of this friction slows down moving objects. Eventually, they will stop moving unless some force is applied to keep them going.

APPLYING WHAT YOU HAVE LEARNED

When a car moves ahead, the force from its wheels moving forward is greater than the opposing force of friction — the rubbing of the tires against the roadway.

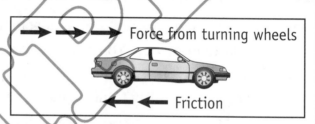

Name two other examples from everyday life in which some force leads to changes in an object's speed or direction.

A. _____

B. _____

WHAT FRICTION DEPENDS ON

The amount of friction depends on the type of surfaces that are rubbing against each other. When surfaces are smooth, they move against each other more easily. **Friction** is greater between rough surfaces. In order to reduce friction in the moving parts of machines, scientists and engineers use oil and other lubricants. These lubricants make rubbing surfaces smoother.

However, not all friction is bad. In fact, friction can be very helpful. If you have ever tried to run on a wet floor, you know that too little friction can make you slip and slide. You need friction to get a grip while moving.

APPLYING WHAT YOU HAVE LEARNED

★ Which has more friction: a roadway before or during a heavy rainfall?

_____ Explain your answer. _____

_____

_____

ENERGY

Where does force come from? Force is actually created by energy. Energy is harder to think about than matter. You cannot always see energy, but you can sometimes feel it. Some days you may feel more energetic than others. You feel like doing things. **Energy** is an ability to do work. It has the power to cause changes in matter. There are many kinds of energy. These include:

| Electricity | Heat | Light | Sound |

Let's take a closer look at each of these forms of energy.

HEAT

Heat is caused by the movement of tiny particles in matter. As the particles in an object move more quickly, the object heats up. **Temperature** measures how fast these particles are moving. For example, water particles are moving faster at 100°C (*its boiling point*) than at 0°C (*its freezing point*).

Heat can pass from one object to other objects. The moving particles in one piece of matter bump into the particles of neighboring matter and speed them up. Heat therefore transfers from hotter objects to colder ones.

If you stir a pot of soup on the stove with a metal spoon, the spoon will get hot after a few minutes. Heat energy has passed from the hot soup to the spoon.

Metal spoon

APPLYING WHAT YOU HAVE LEARNED

★ Identify another example in which heat passes from one object to another object.

_____

LIGHT

Light is another form of energy. Light energy can move through water, air, and glass. Light can even move through empty space. **Solar energy** is a form of light energy. This light energy comes from the sun and travels millions of miles through space to reach Earth.

ELECTRICITY

Electricity is a third form of energy. Electricity can flow easily through many types of materials. It is based on the movement of charges from one particle to the next. Most metals are good conductors of electricity.

APPLYING WHAT YOU HAVE LEARNED

★ Identify two ways that you have used electricity today.

1. _____   2. _____

ELECTRICAL CIRCUITS

Electricity can flow in a **circuit**. An electrical circuit is a system with several parts:

A source that provides electricity	Something that uses electricity	Wires to carry the electricity

A battery is one type of source that produces electrical energy. Every battery has a positive (+) and a negative (-) side. Wires connected to the battery carry the electricity (*also known as electric current*). However, the electricity will only move if the wires and other parts form a **complete circuit**. This gives a continuous path for the electricity to move through.

For example, imagine a simple circuit with a light bulb at one end and a battery at the other (Figure 1). Electricity leaves one side of the battery and moves through a wire to the light bulb. The electricity then moves through the light bulb. The light bulb uses the electrical energy to light up. The electricity then continues moving through the wire back to the battery.

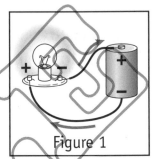

Figure 1

If the circuit is cut at any point, the electricity moving around the circuit will stop (Figure 2). As a result, the light will have no electricity flowing into it, and it will go out.

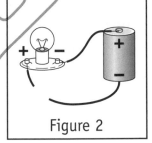

Figure 2

The wires must also be connected to opposite sides of the battery. If both ends of the wire are connected to the same side of the battery, the electricity will not move around the circuit (Figure 3). The bulb will receive no energy and will not go on.

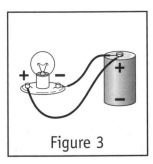

Figure 3

If both ends of the wire are connected to the same side of the light bulb, the electricity will go around the circuit without going through the light bulb (Figure 4). Again, the bulb will not light up.

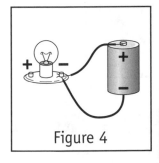

Figure 4

For an electrical appliance like a toaster to work, there must also be a complete path from the power source to the appliance, through its parts, and back to the power source.

APPLYING WHAT YOU HAVE LEARNED

Each circuit below has light bulbs, a battery as a source of power, and wires.

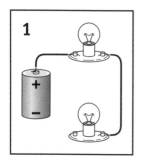 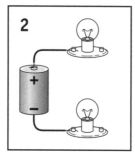 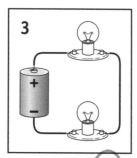 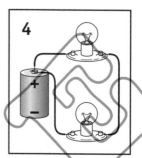

★ In which circuit will the light bulbs go on? _____

★ Why won't the other circuits light the bulbs? _____

_____

_____

TYPES OF CIRCUITS

There are two main types of circuits — *series* and *parallel*.

SERIES CIRCUIT

In a **series circuit**, light bulbs, wires, and a source of electricity are connected along a single path. If any part of the series circuit is cut, electricity can no longer flow through any of the circuit. For example, if there is a broken bulb in the circuit below, the entire series of lights will not work until the broken bulb has been replaced.

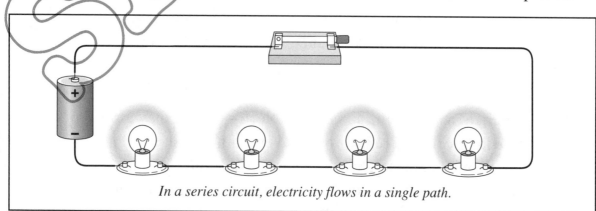

In a series circuit, electricity flows in a single path.

PARALLEL CIRCUIT

In a **parallel circuit**, light bulbs, wires, and a source of electricity are connected by several pathways. If any part of the parallel circuit is cut, electricity can still continue to run through the rest of the circuit.

APPLYING WHAT YOU HAVE LEARNED

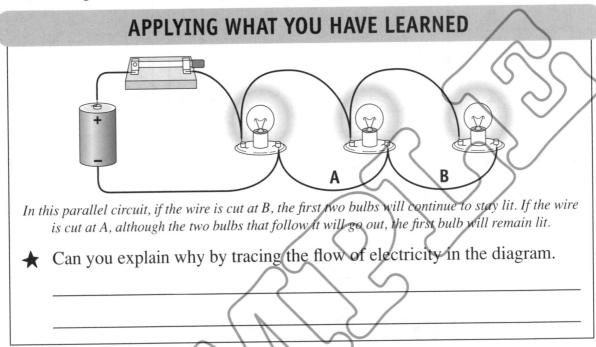

In this parallel circuit, if the wire is cut at B, the first two bulbs will continue to stay lit. If the wire is cut at A, although the two bulbs that follow it will go out, the first bulb will remain lit.

★ Can you explain why by tracing the flow of electricity in the diagram.

_____

_____

On-Off Switches. In both series and parallel circuits, there may be an on-off **switch**. This switch makes it easy to cut the circuit. When the on-off switch in a series circuit is turned off, nothing in the series will be on. When an on-off switch is turned off in a parallel circuit, some or all of the circuit may be off, based on the location of the switch.

SPECIAL PROPERTIES OF ELECTRICITY

Electricity has several important properties. When electricity runs through a wire, the wire becomes **magnetic**. When electricity runs through some materials, it can make them hot. For example, irons, toasters, and electric heaters all produce heat when electricity runs through them.

A few materials will become so hot with electricity that they glow. You can see this in a light bulb. Electricity runs through a very thin wire at the center of the bulb. The wire gets so hot it begins to glow. The gases inside the bulb then become bright. Appliances making use of these properties — bulbs, alarms, irons, or buzzers — can be connected in either a series or parallel circuit.

APPLYING WHAT YOU HAVE LEARNED

★ Examine the electrical appliances illustrated below. Identify what kind of energy each appliance produces.

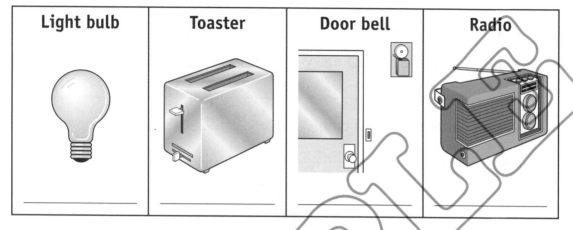

Light bulb	Toaster	Door bell	Radio

SOUND ENERGY

Sound is created by vibrating objects. For example, when a person plucks at a guitar string, the string begins to vibrate. The energy from the vibrating string causes the air to vibrate. Our ears are very sensitive to these vibrations. The energy from these vibrations of air passes to our ears, and we hear these vibrations as sound.

When vibrations are stronger, their sound is **louder**. When vibrations are faster, their sound is higher. When they are slower, their sound is lower. How high or low a sound appears is known as its **pitch**. Sound travels in waves in all directions from its source. If it hits an object like a wall, the sound may bounce off, or **reflect** away from this object.

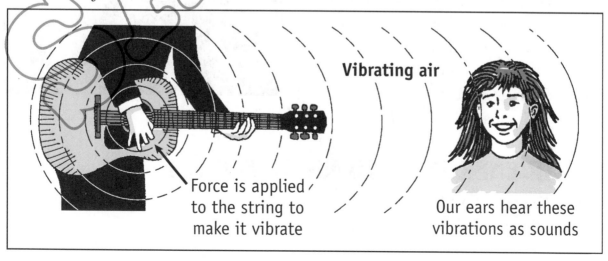

Vibrating air

Force is applied to the string to make it vibrate

Our ears hear these vibrations as sounds

APPLYING WHAT YOU HAVE LEARNED

1. How does the loudness of a sound differ from its pitch? _____
_____

2. If you put your ear on the wall, it is sometimes possible to pick up what is being said in the next room. Why is this so? _____
_____

3. Can sound travel through empty space? _____ Why or why not?
_____
_____

ENERGY CHANGES

Energy can change its form. The examples below illustrate how this works:

ELECTRICAL ENERGY → LIGHT ENERGY

Electricity may flow through a material that gets very hot. The material can get so hot that it glows. In this example, electrical energy becomes light energy.

SOLAR ENERGY → HEAT ENERGY

We use the sun's energy in different ways almost every day. For example, you might hang laundry outside to use the sun's heat to dry clothes. If you go to the beach and lie in the sun, you will start to feel hot. The energy from the sun — solar energy — is heating your body. In this example, solar energy changes into heat energy.

SOLAR ENERGY → CHEMICAL ENERGY

Plants change energy from the sun into chemical energy. This chemical energy is stored in the plants.

THE FLOW OF ENERGY

It is often possible to trace how energy flows through an object or a system:

A LIGHT BULB

A battery changes its chemical energy into electrical energy. This electricity runs through a circuit into a light bulb. A small wire in the bulb gets so hot that it glows. Some of the electricity changes into light energy. If you put your hand close to the light bulb, your hand will feel heat. Some of the light energy has changed into heat energy.

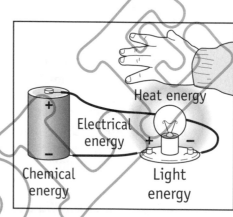

| CHEMICAL ENERGY | → | ELECTRICAL ENERGY | → | LIGHT ENERGY | → | HEAT ENERGY |

EATING FOOD

When we eat, we take chemical energy into our bodies. We later change this chemical energy into the energy needed to move our bodies. Later in this book,

| CHEMICAL ENERGY | → | ENERGY OF MOTION |

you will learn how energy flows through an entire ecosystem (*ecological system*).

WHAT YOU SHOULD KNOW

☐ You should know that motion consists of speed and direction. When force is applied to an object, it changes its motion. Gravity, pushes and pulls, magnetism, and friction are common forces.

☐ You should know that energy has the ability to change or move matter. There are many kinds of energy, such as heat, light and electricity.

☐ You should know that electricity flows in a circuit. Electricity can produce heat, light, sound and magnetic effects.

☐ You should know that a vibrating object can produce sound. Sounds have special characteristics like loudness and pitch.

LESSON STUDY CARDS

Position and Motion

★ **Position.** Position is where an object is located in relation to other things.

★ **Motion** occurs when an object changes its position. Motion includes speed and direction.

- **Speed.** Speed measures the distance an object travels in a given amount of time, such as kilometers (km) per hour.
- **Direction.** The path or route an object takes. Objects may go in straight, up-and-down, or in a circular motion.

Force

Force is what makes an object change its speed or direction.

★ **Friction** is a force created by the rubbing of two surfaces. On Earth, friction slows down moving objects.

★ **Gravity.** The force pulling objects to Earth. The force of gravity increases with the mass of the object.

★ **Push-Pull Force.** The force created when an object hits another object.

★ **Magnetic Force.** A force from a magnet pulling at some metals.

Energy

Energy is something with an ability to change matter. There are many forms of energy:

★ **Electricity.** Energy that often runs in circuits.

★ **Heat.** Energy of particles in matter move faster as they heat up.

★ **Light.** Can travel through space and many materials.

★ **Sound.** Energy carried by vibrations in the air or other matter.

The Flow of Energy

Energy can change its form. Here are some common examples:

★ **Light Bulb.** A battery changes chemical energy into electrical energy. This electricity flows through a circuit. The electricity then causes the bulb to light up, becoming light energy.

★ **Eating Food.** We take food into our bodies with chemical energy. Our bodies change this into the energy needed to move our bodies.

CHECKING YOUR UNDERSTANDING

1. Jack arranged wires, a battery, a switch and a light bulb in four different ways as shown below. Which bulb will light up?

S4.C 2.1.3

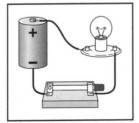
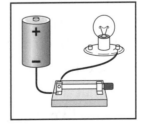
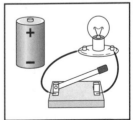

A   B   C   D

HINT   *To answer this question correctly, you must understand electrical circuits. In a circuit, electricity leaves the source and travels around a pathway until it returns to the other side of the source. Only **Choice B** will create a closed circuit when the switch is closed.*

Now answer some other questions on your own. Circle the correct answer.

2. If the person in the picture lets go of the rope, the weight (*w*) will fall to the ground. What force is pulling the weight to the ground?

    A   magnetism
    B   friction
    C   gravity
    D   electricity

    S4.C
    3.1.1

3. A student measures the time it took her to run 5 kilometers (km). What is she able to calculate using her distance and time measurements?

    A   mass
    B   speed
    C   force
    D   temperature

    S4.A
    1.3.1

4. Which tools are needed to measure the speed of a penny sliding across a table?

    A   stopwatch, ruler
    B   balance, ruler
    C   thermometer, stopwatch
    D   thermometer, balance

    S4.A
    2.2.1

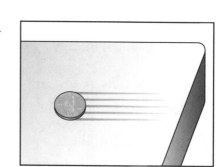

5. A student watches cars race around an oval track. What type of motion will the student observe?

    A   up and down
    B   back and forth
    C   straight and circular
    D   side-to-side

    S4.C
    3.1.2

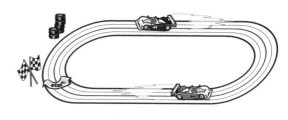

6. Sound is created when someone plucks on the strings of a violin. The shorter strings will vibrate faster than the longer ones. What happens as the vibrations of the violin strings become faster?

A   The sound becomes louder.

B   The sound becomes softer

C   The pitch gets higher.

D   The pitch gets lower.

S4.C
2.1.4

7. What force slows down a ball rolling on the ground?

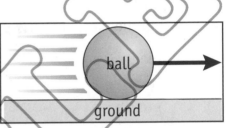

A   magnetism

B   light

C   heat

D   friction

S4.C
3.1.1

8. A student goes out for a walk and sees a flash of lightning in the night sky. What does this flash of lightning show?

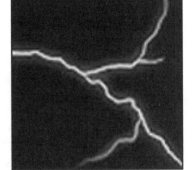

A   Lightning is not dangerous.

B   Electricity flows in a circuit.

C   Light is a form of heat.

D   Electrical energy can change into light.

S4.C
2.1.1

9. Which two forms of energy are released by these burning candles?

A   light and heat

B   sound and chemical

C   magnetic and light

D   electrical and magnetic

S4.C
2.1.2

10. Which form of energy can travel by vibrating particles of air?

A   electrical energy

B   light energy

C   magnetic energy

D   sound energy

S4.C
2.1.1

11. What happens to sound that bounces off a smooth, shiny surface?

A   It is interrupted.

B   It is reflected.

C   It is absorbed.

D   It is stopped.

♦ **Examine the Question**
♦ **Recall What You Know**
♦ **Apply What You Know**

S4.C
2.1.4

12. The graph on the right shows the movement of a car during a 4-hour trip. What was the speed of the car if it traveled at the same speed for all four hours?

A   0 km per hour

B   50 km per hour

C   100 km per hour

D   200 km per hour

S4.A
1.3.1

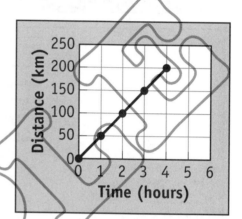

Use the information in the table to answer question 13.

Time of Day	Total Distance Traveled
8:00 AM	0 miles
9:00 AM	30 miles
10:00 AM	60 miles
11:00 AM	90 miles

13. A student went on a car trip with her family. In her diary, she recorded the time of day and how far her family had traveled since they began their trip.

Part A: What speed is the student's family traveling in miles per hour?

S4.A
1.3.1

_____

Part B: Identify one type of force that affects the motion of her family's car.

S4.C
3.1.1

_____

_____

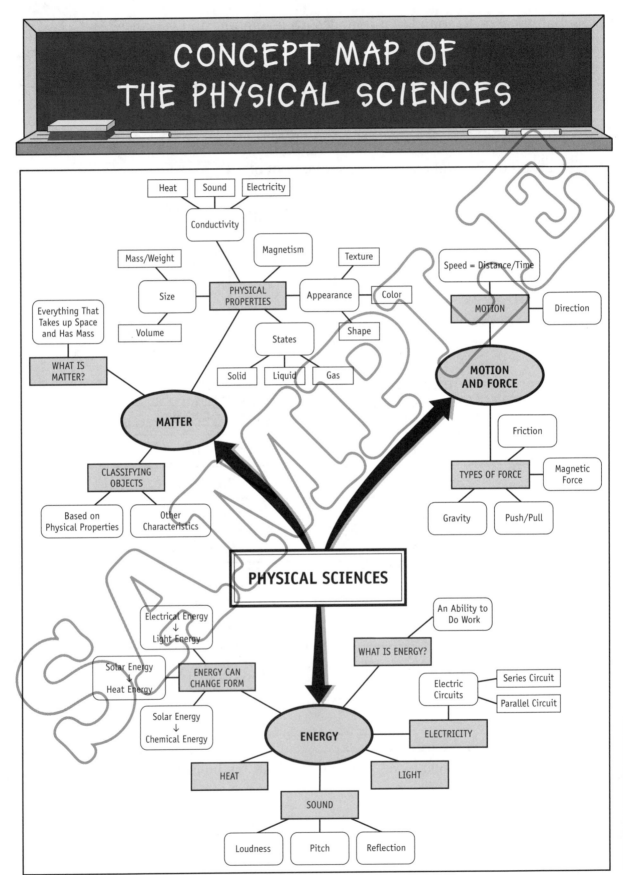

CONCEPT MAP OF
THE PHYSICAL SCIENCES

TESTING YOUR UNDERSTANDING

1. A group of students is asked to classify the objects on the list to the right. Which physical property can be used to classify the objects into only two groups?

    A   magnetism

    B   color

    C   states of matter

    D   mass

    S4.C 1.1.2

    ○   List of Objects
    • water
    • milk
    • chocolate bar
    ○ • apple

2. Students in a class examine an iron pot. Which **best** describes this pot?

    A   It has a soft texture.

    B   It conducts heat well.

    C   It is not attracted to a magnet.

    D   It may melt on a warm day.

    S4.C 1.1.1

3. A student lives near an airport. Whenever a plane flies over his house, his house windows shake. Which **best** explains why this happens?

    A   Energy from the sound vibrations makes the windows shake.

    B   Heat from the airplane engines makes the windows shake.

    C   Magnetism from the airplane makes the windows shake.

    D   Light bouncing off the airplane makes the windows shake.

    S4.C 2.1.4

4. Which appliance below changes electrical energy into light energy?

    S4.C 2.1.2

      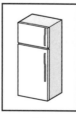

    A   B   C   D

5. A student picks up a trumpet and blows into the mouthpiece. How does blowing on the trumpet cause sound?

A   The trumpet heats the air.
B   The air in the trumpet vibrates.
C   The trumpet cools the air.
D   The air in the trumpet disappears.

S4.C
2.1.4

6. Mr. James mops the floors in the school each afternoon. When he finishes mopping, he always puts up a sign stating, "Warning: Floor Slippery When Wet." Which force is reduced when the floor is wet?

A   heat
B   friction
C   collision
D   magnetism

S4.C
3.1.1

7. A student is given a question to answer for science homework. The question asks why air is matter. What should she write as her answer?

A   Air is invisible.
B   Air takes up space and has mass.
C   Air is needed for people to breathe.
D   Air takes the shape of its container.

S4.C
1.1.1

8. A student measured the temperature of water in a glass on a window ledge in the early morning and late afternoon. She did this for seven days. Each day, she observed the water temperature was higher in the late afternoon than in the morning. Which type of energy was she measuring?

A   heat energy
B   light energy
C   electrical energy
D   chemical energy

S4.C
2.1.1

9. A teacher seeks to complete the circuit to turn on both light bulbs. Where should the teacher connect a wire to turn on both light bulbs A and B?

    A   between point 1 and point 2
    B   between point 1 and point 7
    C   between point 4 and point 6
    D   between point 2 and point 6

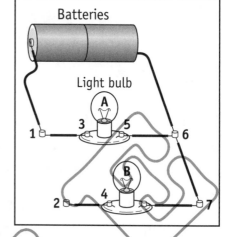

10. Scientists often describe the position of an object by locating it relative to other objects.

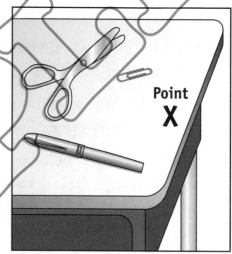

Part A: Make one factual statement that describes the relative location of the scissors on the desktop.

S4.C
3.1.3

_____

_____

Part B: If a strong magnet is placed on the desk at point X, what motion will occur to the objects on the desk?

S4.C
3.1.1

_____

_____

CHECKLIST OF ELIGIBLE CONTENT

Directions. Now that you have completed this unit, place a check (✔) next to those objectives you understand. If you are having trouble recalling information about any of these objectives, review the chapter in the accompanying brackets.

☐ **S4.C.1.1.1** You should be able to use physical properties [e.g., shape, size, volume, color, magnetism, state (i.e., solid and gas), conductivity (i.e., heat)] to describe matter. [**Lesson 11**]

☐ **S4.C.1.1.2** You should be able to categorize or group objects using their physical characteristics. [**Lesson 11**]

☐ **S4.C.2.1.1** You should be able to identify energy forms, energy transfer, and energy examples (e.g., light, heat, electrical). [**Lesson 12**]

☐ **S4.C.2.1.2** You should be able to describe the flow of energy through an object or system (e.g., feeling radiant heat from a light bulb, eating food to get energy, using a battery to light a bulb or run a fan). [**Lesson 12**]

☐ **S4.C.2.1.3** You should be able to recognize or illustrate simple direct current series and parallel circuits composed of batteries, light bulbs (or other common loads), wire, and on/off switches. [**Lesson 12**]

☐ **S4.C.2.1.4** You should be able to identify characteristics of sound (e.g., pitch, loudness, reflection). [**Lesson 12**]

☐ **S4.C.3.1.1** You should be able to describe changes in motion caused by forces (e.g., magnetic, pushes or pulls, gravity, friction). [**Lesson 12**]

☐ **S4.C.3.1.2** You should be able to compare the relative movement of objects or describe types of motion that are evident forces (e.g., bouncing ball, moving in a straight line, back and forth, merry-go-round). [**Lesson 12**]

☐ **S4.C.3.1.3** You should be able to describe the position of an object by locating it relative to another object or a stationary background (e.g., geographic direction, left, up). [**Lesson 12**]

EARTH AND SPACE SCIENCES

In this unit, you will learn how Earth's landforms and bodies of water were created, and how Earth's resources are used.

You will also learn about weather conditions, how they are measured, and the instruments used to measure them. Finally, you will learn about our planet and its relationship to the sun and the moon.

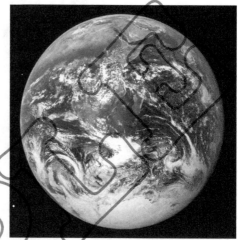

A view of our planet, Earth, from space.

★ **Lesson 13: Earth's Landforms and Resources.** In this lesson, you will learn about landforms and water sources found in Pennsylvania, such as mountains, valleys, lakes and caves. You will also learn about Earth's resources, such as water and soil, and how humans benefit from their use.

★ **Lesson 14: Weather and Space.** In this lesson, you will learn about basic weather conditions and how they are measured. You will also learn about the motions of Earth and the moon in space.

KEY TERMS YOU WILL LEARN ABOUT IN THIS UNIT

- Glaciers
- Water Erosion
- Sinkholes
- Salt Water
- Fresh Water
- Pond
- Bay
- River
- Wetland
- Watershed
- Groundwater
- Atmosphere
- Barometer
- Weather
- Rotate
- Axis
- Orbit
- Moon

LESSON 13

EARTH'S LANDFORMS AND RESOURCES

In this lesson, you will learn about Earth's landforms, water sources, and resources.

— IMPORTANT IDEAS —

A. Changes in Earth's natural history created different **landforms** in Pennsylvania. These include **mountains**, **valleys**, **caves**, and **sinkholes**.

B. **Fresh water** is usually found in **lakes**, **rivers**, **streams**, **creeks**, **watersheds**, and **wetlands**. **Salt water** is usually found in **oceans** and **bays**.

C. Water goes through phase changes, causing the **water cycle**.

D. Earth contains many valuable resources, including **rocks**, **soil** and **water**.

E. Humans benefit from using Earth's resources. These resources can be used to make **renewable**, **nonrenewable** and **reusable** products.

PENNSYLVANIA'S MAJOR LANDFORMS

Landforms are the shapes of Earth's surface. You can think of Pennsylvania as a giant rectangle. Running across the middle of the rectangle, from the southwest (*lower left*) to the northeast (*upper right*), are the **Appalachian Mountains**. These mountains have rich coal resources, but poor soil for farming. To the west (*left*) of these mountains are **ridges** and **valleys**.

Pennsylvania's major landforms include mountains, ridges, and valleys.

192

Layers of sedimentary rock have formed ridges that are 1,000 feet high and separated by valleys many miles long. Farther west is a **plateau** — a flat, high region, or table-top — that runs west to Lake Erie.

Southeast of the Appalachians are the rolling hills of the **Piedmont region**, with some of the most fertile soil in the nation. Finally, the southeastern corner of the state, around Philadelphia, is part of the **Atlantic Coastal Plain**. This area is lower and flatter than the rest of the state.

APPLYING WHAT YOU HAVE LEARNED

★ Look at an atlas or on the Internet for a map of Pennsylvania showing its major landforms. Then fill in the outline map below.

HOW LANDFORMS WERE CREATED

Pennsylvania's landforms were created by processes that took millions of years.

MOUNTAINS

Pennsylvania's mountains were formed by the folding of Earth's **crust** — its outer layer of rock. Layers of rock from opposite directions pushed together. As they pushed, layers of rock folded upwards. Afterwards, part of these ancient mountains were worn down by rain, wind and ice.

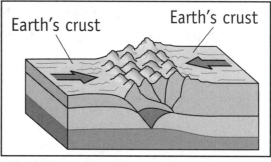

The folding of Earth's crust builds mountains.

GLACIERS

Thousands of years ago, Earth's climate was much colder than it is today. Snows never melted, but froze into ice. The weight of the ice pressed down, making the ice more dense and compact. These rivers of ice, known as **glaciers**, covered parts of Pennsylvania. As the glaciers moved along the surface, they scraped through mountain valleys. When they stopped moving, they deposited the rich soil that now exists in the Piedmont region. As Earth's climate got warmer, the glaciers melted. Their water formed many of Pennsylvania's lakes and rivers.

WATER EROSION

Rainfall on Pennsylvania's mountains falls downhill. Eventually, this running water reaches **valleys**, (*the land between mountains*), and forms **rivers**. These rivers slowly cut through the rock, making the valleys even deeper. **Water erosion** occurs when water carries away bits of rock, soil, and sand.

Valley Creek in Valley Forge National Park, Pennsylvania

CAVES

Caves are large holes in the ground that people can enter. Caves are often formed when rain combines with minerals to form acids. These acids eat away at the rock. Caves can also be formed by bubbles left in molten rock (*lava*) as it cools.

SINKHOLES

Sinkholes are holes in the ground. They are usually formed when groundwater removes soil or rock. If there is not enough support for the land above, then a sudden collapse of the land can occur. Sometimes sinkholes are formed when a cave collapses.

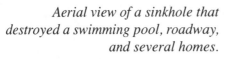

Aerial view of a sinkhole that destroyed a swimming pool, roadway, and several homes.

APPLYING WHAT YOU HAVE LEARNED

Scientists often make models to understand Earth's structures. A model is a replica that represents something else. To make a model of a mountain, you might use clay or papier-maché (*newspaper mixed with paste*). After forming this model, you might paint it. Fill in the boxes below, describing how you would make each model. The first one has been completed for you.

Landform	Making a Model
How would you make a model of a valley?	Use a thick, flat sheet of cardboard. Build two mountains out of clay or paper-maché. Create a long, narrow space between the mountains. Label the space "valley."
How would you make a model of a river or lake?	
A **peninsula** is land surrounded by water on three sides. How would you make a model of a peninsula?	
A **watershed** is an area that drains all the water that reaches it as rainfall. How would you make a model of a watershed?	

Your teacher may now want to divide your class into groups. Each group should choose one of the landforms listed above. Following the instructions in the chart you have made, create an actual model of the landform you selected.

SOURCES OF WATER

Three-quarters of Earth's surface is covered with water. Most of this water is in the world's oceans. The water in the oceans contains salt and other minerals. Because of its salty taste, ocean water is known as **salt water**.

The water found in lakes, rivers, ponds, and streams comes from rain. It is known as **fresh water**. Most fish that live in fresh water cannot survive in saltwater. Saltwater fish, from the oceans, cannot live in fresh water.

A variety of water bodies can be found in Pennsylvania:

- ★ **Pond.** A pond is a small, shallow body of fresh water. Sunlight reaches its bottom.

- ★ **Lake.** A lake is a large, deep, inland body of water. Most lakes hold fresh water. Lake temperatures change slowly. The northwest border of Pennsylvania borders on **Lake Erie**, one of the Great Lakes. Rivers and streams may flow into and out of a lake, but the water changes slowly. Both ponds and lakes are **lentic systems**.

Lake Erie is the shallowest of the Great Lakes.

- ★ **Bay.** A bay is an area of water, usually coming from the ocean or sea. It is surrounded on three sides by land. A large freshwater lake can have bays.

- ★ **River.** A river is a waterway that carries water from higher places, like mountains, to lower places. The river has banks on each side, and a riverbed that carries the water. Often, rivers carry water to lakes, wetlands, and oceans. Because of its strong current, a river is a **lotic system** (*see page 130*). **Streams** and **creeks** are like small rivers. Often they are found in mountains and hills. They carry water to a larger river. Important rivers in Pennsylvania include the Delaware, Susquehanna, and Ohio Rivers.

- ★ **Wetland.** A wetland is an area of land that is frequently flooded with water, such as a marsh or swamp. The soil is wet but the water is not as deep as in a lake. Special plants and animals, used to swamp-like conditions, live in wetlands. Most wetlands have fresh water, but wetlands along ocean coastlines can be flooded with salt water from the ocean.

- ★ **Watershed.** A watershed is an area of land that collects water from rainfall and drains this water as a unit. The watershed has streams that connect to rivers as they carry surface

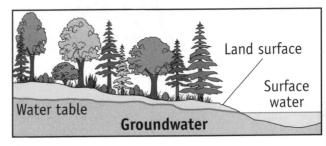

water. When water soaks into the ground, it sinks below until it finally hits a hard surface of rock. The water then collects as **groundwater** and flows through porous rock or in underground streams.

THE ROLE OF WETLANDS AND WATERSHEDS

Wetlands and watersheds serve many important roles. They store large amounts of fresh water. They also act to clean, or **filter**, this water. As water sinks into the ground, it passes through layers of sand, gravel, and rock. Impurities are removed from the water. Wetlands also act to filter water as the water flows slowly through them.

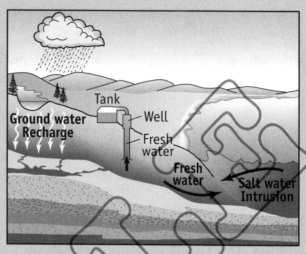

By digging wells and pumping water to the surface, farmers can use groundwater to irrigate crops. However, they must be careful not to use all the groundwater in the watershed. It takes time for water from rain to collect as groundwater. Farmers therefore must allow for **groundwater recharge** — the replacement of groundwater — when they pump groundwater from wells for their crops.

APPLYING WHAT YOU HAVE LEARNED

How does Earth filter water?

Take a large, empty plastic soda bottle. Have your parent cut the bottle in half. Place a cloth around the opening of the top half. Put a tight rubber band around it to secure it in place on the bottle. Turn the top half upside down. Put it in the bottom half of the bottle. Fill the opening with a layer of tiny rocks or gravel. Fill the rest of the bottle with a layer of fine sand. Pour muddy water into the funnel top of the bottle. See what the water looks like as it drips through.

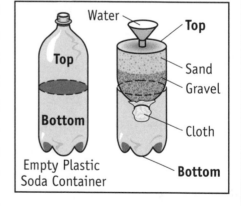

Record your observations: _____

_____

APPLYING WHAT YOU HAVE LEARNED

Can you match the correct body of water with its definition?

1.	Bay _____	A	A swampy area in which the soil is usually wet
2.	Lake _____	B	Water with minerals found in the ocean
3.	Lentic System _____	C	A small body of water with little movement
4.	Lotic System _____	D	Any system of water with little movement
5.	Pond _____	E	An area of land that drains water together
6.	River _____	F	Area of water surrounded by land on 3 sides
7.	Salt Water _____	G	A large body of inland water
8.	Watershed _____	H	Any system of flowing water
9.	Wetland _____	I	A fast-moving body of water, carrying water from a high place to a lower one.

EARTH'S RESOURCES

Earth contains many different resources. These include rocks, soils, fossil fuels, and water.

ROCKS

A **rock** is any solid found in Earth's crust or below that is made of one or more minerals. Many minerals form geometric shapes known as **crystals**. Scientists often classify rocks based on their color, size, shape, hardness, mineral crystals, and how the rock was formed. Much of Earth consists of hard, dense rock or molten (*melted*) material made from rock. As you go deeper into Earth, the temperature rises and the rock becomes molten.

SOIL

Some people just call it "dirt," but **soil** is important for our survival. Soil is needed for growing crops to feed humans and animals. It is important for plants because soil stores nutrients and supports plant roots and stems.

Soil is needed to grow crops to feed our growing population.

The actions of the wind, rainfall, streams and rivers, ice and changing temperatures break down rocks into tiny pieces. The particles of weathered rock mix with decaying plants and animals and their waste products. Soil is therefore a mixture of many materials, including sand, clay, rock, water, fungi, bacteria, and decayed plants and animals. There are different types of soil based on the mix of materials found in each type. Each type of soil has its own texture or feel, its own ability to hold water, and its own ability to support life.

Soil texture is based on how large the pieces of clay and other particles in the soil are, and how much decayed plant and animal life there is. Soils also contain different chemicals, like salts. These chemicals affect the ability of soil to support life. Farmers may add more dead plant and animal material (*humus*) or special chemicals to the soil to help crops grow.

APPLYING WHAT YOU HAVE LEARNED

★ What role does soil play in helping to maintain life on Earth? _____

_____

_____

FOSSIL FUELS

Fossil fuels — like coal, oil, and natural gas — are very special resources. They are usually found in deposits beneath Earth's surface. Fossil fuels can be burned to release large amounts of energy. We burn fossil fuels to run our car engines, heat our homes, power our machinery, and create electricity. They can also be used to create new materials, like synthetic fibers. Fossil fuels actually come from the remains of ancient living things.

★ **Coal** is a brown or black rock formed from plants in ancient forests and swamps as long as 400 million years ago.

★ **Oil and natural gas** are also fossil fuels. They were formed by billions of tiny animals and algae in the ocean. Over millions of years, heat and pressure changed their bodies into liquid oil and natural gas.

OIL (PETROLEUM) AND NATURAL GAS FORMATION

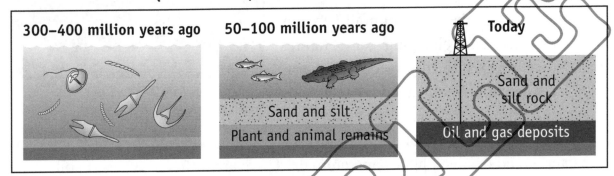

WATER

Water is another important resource. People enjoy using water for agriculture, energy and recreation. We drink, cook, and wash with water. Farmers use water to help their crops and livestock grow. We use waterfalls to turn turbines in power plants to produce hydroelectricity. We also use water to carry sewage out to sea, and for transportation. Finally, we enjoy the recreation that water provides — boating, swimming, and fishing. Because water has so many uses, it is important to conserve water supplies and to prevent pollution of one of our most important resources.

THE WATER CYCLE

You know that water can exist in different **states** — as a **solid**, **liquid**, and **gas**. The **water cycle** is the process by which Earth's water moves into and out of the atmosphere as it changes its state. The water cycle begins when energy from the sun heats the surface of lakes and oceans. This solar energy causes some of the water to **evaporate**. The liquid water turns into an invisible gas, **water vapor**. This water vapor rises into the atmosphere. In Earth's atmosphere, the water vapor cools and **condenses**, or turns back into tiny droplets of liquid water (*condensation*). These droplets are so light that they remain floating in the atmosphere, where they form clouds. When the droplets get larger and heavier, they fall to the ground as raindrops. If it is cold, this water freezes and falls as snow, sleet, or hail (*precipitation*).

Gravity pulls this rain, snow or hail down to under the ground. Some of it falls on land, where it forms lakes and rivers. Some of the water is absorbed by the ground. It sinks until it hits dense rock and collects as **groundwater**. Most of the precipitation either falls on the oceans or gradually drains back into them. The process then begins all over again, as surface water evaporates into the atmosphere.

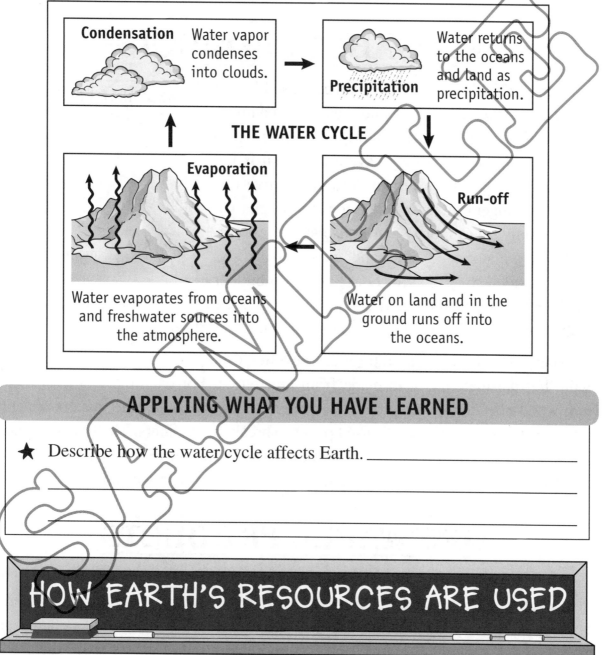

APPLYING WHAT YOU HAVE LEARNED

★ Describe how the water cycle affects Earth. _____

_____

_____

HOW EARTH'S RESOURCES ARE USED

Earth's materials — its rocks, minerals, plants, animals, soil, water and fossil fuels — are used to make products that help people meet their needs.

These products can be divided into three types:

  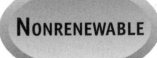

REUSABLE PRODUCTS

Some products, like glass bottles, can be reused. These bottles are collected, washed, and reused by manufacturers to hold drinks or other products. Clothing is also a reusable product. You may have a shirt that is too small because you have grown. You could give this shirt to a younger brother or sister or even to a charity. This not only saves money, but it also saves resources. Building materials — like sand, gravel, rocks, and bricks — can also be reused. For example, a builder may knock down a building. The builder then uses the bricks from this building to build a new fireplace.

Many products are reused through **recycling**. The product itself cannot be used again, but the materials it is made from are reused. For example, paper is made from wood fibers known as pulp. Newspapers, cardboard, and other papers are collected. Water is mixed with this used paper to break up the fibers. The fibers are then washed, bleached, and reused to make new **recycled paper**. Some plastics are also recycled. The plastic is collected, melted, and remade into new plastic products.

RENEWABLE PRODUCTS

A **renewable resource** is one that can be regrown again to replace what has been used. Renewable products include foods. For example, corn crops are cut down and sent to markets for people to buy. The next year, farmers grow new stalks of corn on the same field. As long as people don't eat more corn than farmers grow, the product can be renewed. Other renewable products include lumber (*from trees*), cotton clothes (*from cotton plants*), bread (*made of flour from ground-up wheat*), and hamburgers (*made of beef from cattle*).

NONRENEWABLE PRODUCTS

Not all products are reusable or renewable. Some products can only be used once. **Nonrenewable products** include products made from minerals and fossil fuels (*coal and oil*). Gasoline, used as fuel to power cars, comes from oil. Once it is burned, this gasoline cannot be used again. For this reason, it is important to conserve energy from fossil fuels. Oil is also used to make most plastics and synthetic fabrics. Did you know that rayon, nylon, and polyester are all fabrics made of different types of plastic? If these products are not reused or recycled, they cannot be renewed.

APPLYING WHAT YOU HAVE LEARNED

★ Classify each of the following products by checking the correct box:

	Recyclable	Renewable	Nonrenewable
Glass bottle	☐	☐	☐
Coal	☐	☐	☐
Lumber	☐	☐	☐
Wool sweater	☐	☐	☐
Gasoline	☐	☐	☐
Plastic bottle	☐	☐	☐

WHAT YOU SHOULD KNOW

☐ You should know that changes in Earth's natural history created different landforms in Pennsylvania. These include mountains, valleys, caves, and sinkholes.

☐ You should know that fresh water is found in lakes, rivers, streams, watersheds, and wetlands. Salt water is found in oceans and most bays.

☐ You should know that Earth contains valuable resources, including soil and water. Water goes through phase changes, causing the water cycle.

☐ You should know that humans benefit from using Earth's resources. These resources can be used to make renewable, nonrenewable and reusable products.

LESSON STUDY CARDS

Earth's Landforms

There are numerous types of landforms:

★ **Mountains.**
★ **Caves.**
★ **Valleys.**
★ **Sinkholes.**

Earth's Bodies of Water

★ **Freshwater:**
  • **Lakes.**   • **Rivers.**   • **Creeks.**
  • **Ponds.**   • **Streams.**   • **Wetlands.**
★ **Saltwater: Oceans, most bays**
★ **Lentic (*still water*) vs. Lotic Systems (*flowing water*)**

Earth's Resources

★ **Rock.** A solid found on or in Earth's crust, made of minerals.
★ **Soil.** Material that comes from ground rock and decayed plant and animal material.
★ **Water.** Used for agriculture, energy, and recreation.
★ **Fossil Fuels.** Coal, oil and gas

Water Cycle

★ **Evaporation.**   ★ **Precipitation.**
★ **Condensation.**   ★ **Run-off.**

CHECKING YOUR UNDERSTANDING

1. Which **best** describes what is happening in the water cycle at D?

   A   Water from the land is returning to the ocean.

   B   Water is evaporating into the atmosphere.

   C   Water from the atmosphere is returning to Earth's surface.

   D   Water vapor in the atmosphere is condensing into clouds.

   S4.D 1.3.2

WATER CYCLE

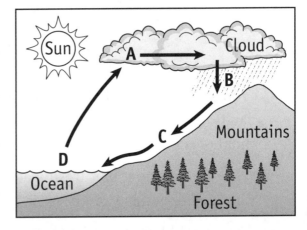

 HINT *To answer this question, you need to be able to understand the water cycle. At point D, the arrow is pointing upwards into the sky. What is happening is that liquid water from the lake is evaporating, and turning into a gas (water vapor). Thus, the correct answer is **Choice B**.*

Now answer some other questions on your own. Circle the correct answer.

2. Which of these products is reusable?

S4.D
1.2.2

 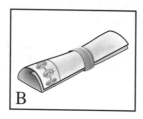  

A   B   C   D

3. Which of these materials used for home building is renewable?

A   oil

B   lumber

C   aluminum

D   copper

◆ **Examine the Question**
◆ **Recall What You Know**
◆ **Apply What You Know**

S4.D
1.2.2

4. A farmer sees an area he believes will be good for farming because of its rich topsoil. Which process contributed most to forming this rich topsoil?

A   sand storms

C   decaying plant life

B   ocean currents

D   folding of Earth's crust

S4.D
1.1.3

5. Which Pennsylvania landform was created by a folding of Earth's crust?

S4.D
1.1.1

Cave   Valley   Sinkhole   Mountain

 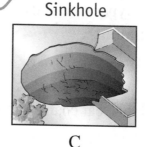 

A   B   C   D

6. A variety of different landforms can be found in Pennsylvania.

S4.D
1.1.1

Part A: Identify one landform found in Pennsylvania today.

_____

Part B: How was the landform you identified in part A created?

_____

_____

LESSON 14

WEATHER AND SPACE

Is it warm or cold outside? Is it sunny, raining, or snowing today? Weather is important because it greatly affects our everyday lives. In this lesson, you will learn about the weather. You will also learn about our planet's position and motion in space.

— IMPORTANT IDEAS —

A. Earth is surrounded by a blanket of air, known as the **atmosphere**. Air takes up space and moves around us as wind. Air pressure can be measured with an instrument called a **barometer**.

B. **Weather** describes conditions in Earth's atmosphere. These conditions include **temperature**, **wind**, **wind speed** and **direction**, **precipitation** and **barometric pressure**. All of these conditions can be measured. Tables, graphs, and maps are used to record information about the weather.

C. Different types of clouds usually accompany different kinds of weather. There are four types of clouds you should know: **cirrus**, **cumulus**, **stratus**, and **cumulonimbus**.

D. Earth **rotates** (*spins*) on its axis. This spinning causes us to have day and night. Earth is **tilted** on its **axis** as it orbits around the sun. This tilting explains why the seasons of the year change from spring and summer to fall and winter.

E. Our view of the **moon** changes as it orbits Earth each month.

THE ATMOSPHERE

The **atmosphere** is the blanket of air that surrounds Earth. Earth's atmosphere is mainly made up of nitrogen and oxygen gas. It is the source of the weather. In fact, the **weather** really refers to conditions in Earth's atmosphere.

AIR PRESSURE

Most of the time, we are not aware of the air, but air is always pushing down on us. The weight of the air causes **air pressure** — the force with which the air presses down. Air pressure is not always the same. It changes based on the amount of moisture in the air, how cold or warm the air is, elevation, and other factors. Scientists use an instrument called a **barometer** to measure air pressure. Barometers generally fall into two main groups:

★ Many barometers use mercury and act almost like a mercury thermometer. A glass tube sits in mercury open to the air. Air pressure pushes the mercury up the tube. Air pressure is often measured in **inches of mercury**.

★ A second type of barometer is round in shape. It uses a metal spring, like the spring of a spring scale. Air pressure squeezes the spring. A needle points to the amount of air pressure.

A barometer is a very effective tool to help us predict what type of weather is ahead. For example, when the barometer is steadily rising, we can expect mild weather and clear skies. When the barometer is steadily falling, it indicates that a storm or rain is coming.

APPLYING WHAT YOU HAVE LEARNED

★ What does a barometer measure? _____

_____

★ How does a barometer help predict the weather? _____

_____

_____

_____

MEASURING WEATHER CONDITIONS

To describe the weather, scientists use special instruments to measure conditions:

TEMPERATURE

Scientists use a **thermometer** to measure how hot or cold the air is. They measure this in degrees Celsius (°C) or Fahrenheit (°F)

PRECIPITATION

Scientists use a **rain gauge** to measure in inches or centimeters the amount of rain that has fallen. The rain gauge measures the height of the column of water it captures. The amount of rainfall is important because it indicates how much water is available to farmers and others.

WIND

Scientists measure wind speed with an **anemometer**. The simplest anemometer consists of four cups, each mounted on one end of four arms. The flow of air turns the cups. Measuring the cups' motion over a period of time tells the average wind speed, such as miles per hour. A **weather vane** measures the direction of the wind.

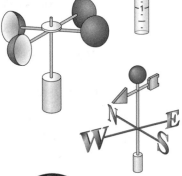

BAROMETRIC PRESSURE

Scientists use a **barometer** to measure air pressure. A change in air pressure helps to predict the weather.

TYPES OF CLOUDS

Clouds are formed by ice and water droplets that have condensed in the atmosphere. The type of cloud cover can often be used to predict the weather.

CIRRUS CLOUDS

Cirrus clouds form out of ice crystals high in the sky. Cirrus clouds tend to look feathery or as a string of

Cirrus Clouds

clouds — appearing thin and white. They usually indicate good weather.

CUMULUS CLOUDS

The word *cumulus* comes from the Latin word for a heap or pile. These clouds can form anywhere. They usually appear as puffy white clouds that look like lumpy tops or large cotton balls with flat bottoms. Cumulus clouds also usually indicate good weather.

Cumulus Clouds

STRATUS CLOUDS

These clouds usually form low in the sky. They often appear as white blankets or layers and can cover the entire sky. When they appear just above the ground, they cause **fog**. Stratus clouds often indicate a gray, dull day with rain.

Stratus Clouds

CUMULONIMBUS CLOUDS

Cumulonimbus clouds form when moist, warm air quickly rises. They often appear as white blankets or mushrooms that reach far upwards. *Nimbus* comes from the word for rain. These clouds often bring heavy rain, thunderstorms, and lightning.

Cumulonimbus Clouds

APPLYING WHAT YOU HAVE LEARNED

★ Based on the cloud formations above, what kind of weather would you predict for each picture? _____

_____

WEATHER DATA

Scientists keep track of the weather by recording weather data on a table, graph, calendar or map. They record the temperature, the direction and speed of the wind, barometric pressure, and precipitation (*rain*, *snow*, and *hail*). Scientists often use special symbols to record this information.

Cloud Cover	Precipitation	Weather Station Information
◯ Clear	•• •• Heavy rain	Wind direction (from north) — Wind speed
⬤ Overcast	✳✳ Heavy snow	Air temperature (°C) (It may also be recorded in °F.) — **18 | 1029** — Air pressure
◖ Partly cloudy	☰ Fog	Cloud cover — Pressure change

A **weather map** is a special kind of map showing weather patterns. Cloud cover, precipitation, wind speed and direction, temperatures and barometric pressure can all be shown on a weather map. This weather map shows that in Ohio it is 20°F, with 1039 air pressure, overcast and winds from the south. Using the symbols on the map, can you tell what the weather is at this time in Pennsylvania?

Weather data can also be recorded in a table or graph. Below is a bar graph showing the average monthly temperature in Philadelphia.

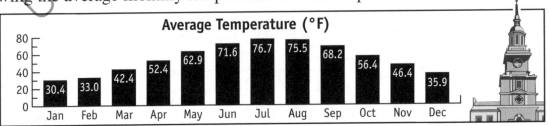

Average Temperature (°F)

Jan	Feb	Mar	Apr	May	Jun	Jul	Aug	Sep	Oct	Nov	Dec
30.4	33.0	42.4	52.4	62.9	71.6	76.7	75.5	68.2	56.4	46.4	35.9

APPLYING WHAT YOU HAVE LEARNED

★ Answer the following questions using the bar graph on page 210.

1. Which month in Philadelphia was the coldest? _____

2. Which month was the warmest? _____

3. What is the average temperature in Philadelphia in April? _____

MOVEMENTS OF EARTH AND THE MOON

Above Earth's atmosphere is space. In space, our planet belongs to the solar system. Earth actually moves through space in two different ways at the same time: it **rotates** on its axis, and it **orbits** the sun.

EARTH'S ROTATION

The Earth **rotates**, or spins, around its **axis** — an imaginary line running through the center of Earth from the North Pole to the South Pole. This rotation takes 24 hours or **one day**. **Night** occurs on that part of Earth that is away from the sun's rays. **Day** occurs on that part of the planet facing the sun. Each morning, the sun appears to rise in the east and set (*go down*) in the west.

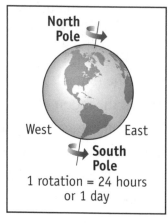

1 rotation = 24 hours or 1 day

EARTH'S REVOLUTION

Earth also **orbits**, or **revolves** around, the sun as it rotates on its axis. The shape of Earth's orbit is slightly **elliptical** — like an oval. It takes just over 365 days for Earth to complete one **orbit** around the sun. One **year** represents the time it takes Earth to orbit the sun.

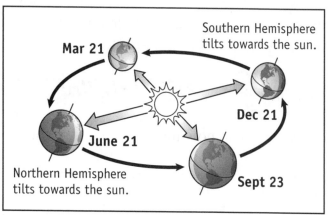

Earth tilts on its **axis** as it orbits the sun. Because of this tilt, the sun's rays hit the Northern Hemisphere more directly in summer than in winter. During summer, days are longer and temperatures are warmer. Because the sun's rays are more direct, shadows are shorter. When it is summer in the Northern Hemisphere, it is winter in the Southern Hemisphere. This is because the Southern Hemisphere tilts away from the sun and receives less direct sunlight at this time. In winter, days are shorter, temperatures are cooler, and shadows are longer. Months later, when it is summer in the Southern Hemisphere, it will be winter in the Northern Hemisphere.

APPLYING WHAT YOU HAVE LEARNED

★ "Earth actually moves in two different ways at one time." Explain this

statement. _____

_____

MOVEMENT OF THE MOON

Earth has one natural satellite, the **moon**. The moon orbits Earth every 29½ days. One **month** is based on how long it takes the moon to orbit Earth. Although we see the moon in the night sky, it does not create its own light. Moonlight is light reflected from the sun. The size of the bright portion of the moon we see changes throughout the month. This

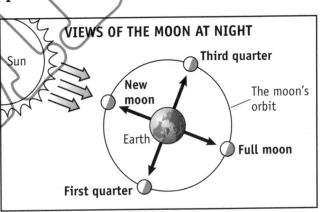

causes the phases of the moon. During a new moon, the moon appears to be completely dark. The moon gradually lights up as a crescent, as a half moon, and finally as a full moon. A full moon is completely lit up. Then it repeats the entire process all over again.

APPLYING WHAT YOU HAVE LEARNED

★ Explain how the movements of the moon and Earth are alike and different.

_____

_____

WHAT YOU SHOULD KNOW

☐ You should know that Earth is surrounded by a blanket of air, known as the atmosphere. Air takes up space and moves around us as wind. Air pressure can be measured with an instrument called a barometer.

☐ You should know that weather describes conditions in Earth's atmosphere. It can be measured based on temperature (*thermometer*), wind speed (*anemometer*), wind direction (*weather vane*), precipitation (*rain gauge*) and air pressure (*barometer*). Tables, graphs, and maps record information about the weather.

☐ You should know that different types of clouds usually accompany different kinds of weather. There are four types of clouds you should know: cirrus, cumulus, stratus, and cumulonimbus.

☐ You should know that Earth rotates (*spins*) on its axis. This spinning causes our day and night. Earth takes one year to orbit the sun. Earth is tilted on its axis as it orbits around the sun. This explains why the seasons of the year change from spring and summer to fall and winter.

☐ You should know that the moon takes about one month to orbit Earth.

LESSON STUDY CARDS

Weather

★ Describes conditions present in the atmosphere.

★ Consists of **barometric pressure** (air pressure), temperature, wind speed and direction, cloud cover and precipitation.

Cloud Types

★ **Cirrus.** High in the atmosphere; appears feathery; indicates fair weather.

★ **Cumulus.** Puffy clouds; indicates fair weather.

★ **Stratus.** Appears as layers, like a blanket; indicates gray sky and probably rain.

★ **Cumulonimbus.** Mushroom-shaped; brings heavy rain, thunderstorms, and lightning.

Earth and Moon

★ **Earth.** Earth rotates on its axis every 24 hours, creating night and day.

• Earth completely orbits around the sun once every year. Earth's orbit around the sun is elliptical (oval).

• Earth's tilt on its axis gives us our four seasons: spring, summer, fall, winter.

★ **Moon.** The moon orbits Earth. It takes about one **month** to complete its orbit. As it orbits, we see different amounts of the moon reflecting the sun's light. This causes the cyclical phases of the moon that we see on Earth.

CHECKING YOUR UNDERSTANDING

1. Which diagram correctly shows the movements of Earth, the sun and the moon?

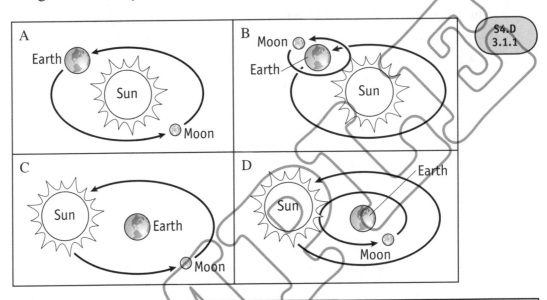

HINT *To answer this question, you need to understand the diagrams and be able to explain the motions of the sun, Earth and moon. The sun is the center of the solar system. Thus, **Choice C** and **Choice D** are wrong. **Choice A** is wrong because Earth and the moon do not move in the same orbit. The moon orbits Earth, so **Choice B** is correct.*

Now answer some other questions on your own. Circle the correct answer.

2. What type of instrument do scientists use to measure air pressure?

   A thermometer
   B barometer
   C rain gauge
   D anemometer

   ♦ Examine the Question
   ♦ Recall What You Know
   ♦ Apply What You Know

   S4.D
   2.1.3

3. A student observes several cumulonimbus clouds in the sky. What is the future weather most likely to be?

   A foggy   B a thunderstorm
   C light rain   D sunny and warm

   S4.D
   2.1.1

4. Which **best** describes the movement of the moon and Earth?

   A   Earth orbits the moon.

   B   The moon orbits Earth.

   C   The sun orbits the moon.

   D   Earth and the moon orbit around each other.

S4.D
3.1.1

5. The illustration to the right shows Earth tilted on its axis. What is an important effect of this tilt?

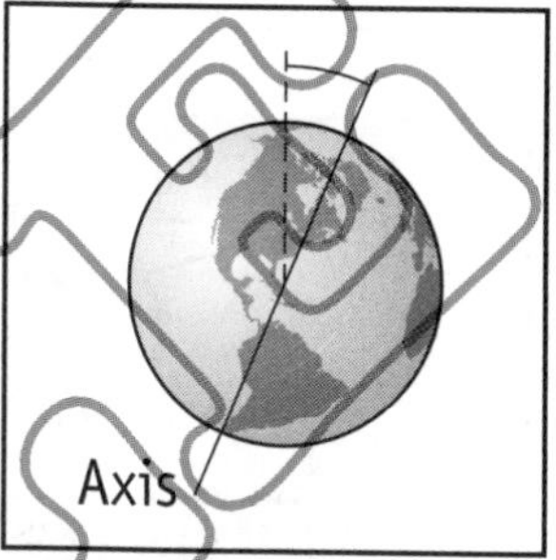

   A   day and night

   B   four seasons

   C   a year of 365 days

   D   phases of the moon

S4.D
3.1.3

Axis

6. Which of these is caused by the turning of the Earth on its axis?

   A   day and night   B   summer and winter

   C   phases of the moon   D   sunlight

S4.D
3.1.2

7. Which weather instrument measures the speed of the wind during a thunder storm?

   A   thermometer   B   anemometer

   C   weather vane   D   barometer

S4.D
2.1.3

8. The barometer is rising. What kind of weather is most likely?

   A   clear skies

   B   rain

   C   thunderstorms

   D   stratus clouds and snow

S4.D
2.1.3

9. Scientists use a rain gauge to measure how much rain has fallen.

S4.D
2.1.3

Part A: Identify one other instrument that measures weather conditions.

_____

Part B: Explain what the instrument you identified in part A measures.

_____

CONCEPT MAP OF THE EARTH AND SPACE SCIENCES

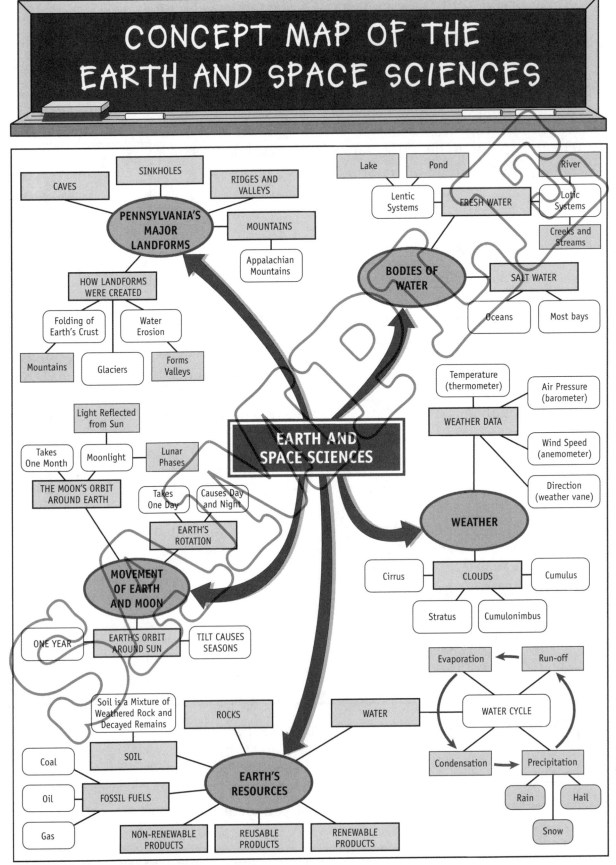

TESTING YOUR UNDERSTANDING

1. Which part of the water cycle came before the X in the diagram?

2. Which of these is a renewable product?

A   gold   B   coal

C   lumber   D   petroleum

3. A student mixes together sand, clay, and decayed material from dead plants. What would this mixture be most useful for learning about?

A   rock   B   soil

C   gas   D   fossils

4. What determines the length of one day on Earth?

A   The time it takes the moon to orbit Earth.

B   The time it takes Earth to orbit the sun.

C   The time it takes Earth to spin one time around its axis.

D   The time it takes Earth to change its tilt on its axis.

5. A class builds a model out of clay and water. The model shows a piece of land surrounded on three sides by water. What does the model represent?

A   stream

B   bay

C   peninsula

D   watershed

S4.D 1.3.2

S4.D 1.2.2

S4.D 1.1.3

S4.D 3.1.2

S4.D 1.1.2

6. Which product is under the wrong heading?

Renewable Products	Reusable Products	Nonrenewable Products
lumber	glass jars	gasoline
wheat	bricks	cotton

A   lumber

C   wheat

B   gasoline

D   cotton

S4.D
1.2.2

Look at the table below to answer question 7.

	Monday	Tuesday	Wednesday	Thursday	Friday
Temperature	75°F	77°F	78°F	80°F	82°F
Barometric Pressure	1030	1020	1010	1000	990

7. Based on the chart, what weather is most likely on Saturday?

A   clear, cool weather

B   warm weather with possible rain

C   cold weather with possible snow

D   hot, humid weather

S4.D
2.1.2

8. What is one way that a watershed affects the environment?

A   It filters and stores water.

B   It condenses water vapor into clouds.

C   It builds mountains and caves.

D   It provides nonrenewable products.

S4.D
1.3.4

9. Weather forecasters study clouds to learn more about weather conditions.

S4.D
2.1.1

Part A: Name and describe one type of cloud.

_____

Part B: Explain what weather conditions are likely with the type of cloud
you identified in part A.

_____

_____

CHECKLIST OF ELIGIBLE CONTENT

☐ **S4.D.1.1.1** You should be able to describe how prominent Earth features in Pennsylvania (e.g., mountains, valleys, caves, sinkholes, lakes, rivers) were formed. **[Lesson 13]**

☐ **S4.D.1.1.2** You should be able to identify various Earth structures (e.g., mountains, watersheds, peninsulas, lakes, rivers, valleys) through the use of models. **[Lesson 13]**

☐ **S4.D.2.1.3** You should be able to describe the composition of soil as weathered rock and decomposed organic remains. **[Lesson 13]**

☐ **S4.D.1.2.1** You should be able to identify products and by-products of plants and animals for human use (e.g., food, clothing, building materials, paper products). **[Lesson 13]**

☐ **S4.D.1.2.2** You should be able to identify the types and uses of Earth materials for renewable, nonrenewable, and reusable products (e.g., human-made products: concrete, paper, plastics, fabrics). **[Lesson 13]**

☐ **S4.D.1.2.3** You should be able to recognize ways that humans benefit from the use of water resources (e.g., agriculture, energy, recreation). **[Lesson 13]**

☐ **S4.D.1.3.1** You should be able to describe types of freshwater and saltwater bodies (e.g., lakes, rivers, wetlands, oceans). **[Lesson 13]**

☐ **S4.D.1.3.2** You should be able to explain how water goes through phase changes (i.e., evaporation, condensation, freezing, melting). **[Lesson 13]**

☐ **S4.D.1.3.4** You should be able to explain the role and relationship of a watershed or a wetland on water sources (e.g., water storage, groundwater recharge, water filtration, water source, water cycle). **[Lesson 13]**

☐ **S4.D.2.1.1** You should be able to identify basic cloud types (i.e., cirrus, cumulus, stratus, and cumulonimbus) and make connections to basic elements of weather (e.g., changes in temperature, precipitation). **[Lesson 14]**

☐ **S4.D.2.1.2** You should be able to identify weather patterns from data charts or graphs of the data (e.g., temperature, wind direction, wind speed, cloud types, precipitation). **[Lesson 14]**

☐ **S4.D.2.1.3** You should be able to identify appropriate instruments (i.e., thermometer, rain gauge, weather vane, anemometer, and barometer) to study weather and what they measure. **[Lesson 14]**

☐ **S4.D.3.1.1** You should be able to describe motions of the Sun — Earth — Moon system. **[Lesson 14]**

☐ **S4.D.3.1.2** You should be able to explain how the motions of the Sun — Earth — Moon system relates to time (e.g., days, months, years). **[Lesson 14]**

☐ **S4.D.3.1.3** You should be able to describe the causes of seasonal change as they relate to the revolution of Earth and the tilt of Earth's axis. **[Lesson 14]**

UNIT 6

A PRACTICE PSSA TEST IN SCIENCE

This unit consists of a complete practice **PSSA Grade 4 Science Test**. Before you begin, you should review a few directions for the test:

★ **Answer All Questions.** This practice test consists of 56 multiple-choice questions, and five short-answer questions.

★ **Use the "E-R-A" Approach.** Remember to **Examine** the question carefully to understand what it is asking. Next, **Recall** what you have learned about that particular topic. Finally, **Apply** your knowledge to answer the question.

★ **Use the Process of Elimination.** When answering a multiple-choice question, it may be clear that certain choices are wrong. Cross out incorrect choices. Select the best response that remains. Never leave a question unanswered.

★ **Revisit Difficult Questions.** If you run into a difficult question, do not be discouraged. Put a check (✔) next to it. Answer it as best you can and move on to other questions. At the end of the test, go back and reread any questions you marked. Sometimes the answer to a question might become clearer to you later.

★ **When You Finish.** When you are finished, check over your work during any time you have left. Do not disturb other students.

Good luck on this practice test!

S4.B.3.1.2

1. Why are green plants in a forest ecosystem important to animals?

    A   They consume food and give off oxygen.

    B   They consume food and give off carbon dioxide.

    C   They produce food and give off oxygen.

    D   They produce food and give off carbon dioxide.

S4.B.1.1.3

2. What needs must every land animal meet to survive?

    A   roots, leaves, and stems

    B   food, water, and air

    C   eyes, nose, and ears

    D   light, soil, and water

S4.A.2.2.1

3. Which tool would a scientist use to measure the temperature of freshly fallen snow?

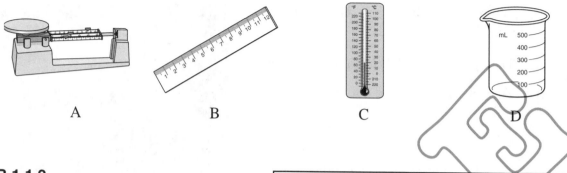

A   B   C   D

S4.B.1.1.2

4. Scientists identify insects as having six legs and three body segments (major parts). Which animal below would be classified as most similar to those in the box on the right?

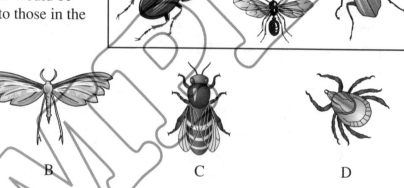

A   B   C   D

S4.A.2.1.1

5. A group of students wants to learn about caterpillars. Which question could **best** be answered by observing caterpillars in a field investigation?

A   How do caterpillars become butterflies?

B   Can caterpillars live without drinking water?

C   How do caterpillars digest food?

D   Will caterpillars grow longer if they are given vitamins?

S4.A.2.1.2

6. A group of students conducts an experiment. They give one rabbit 8 ounces of carrots to eat every day. They give a second rabbit 8 ounces of lettuce. Every week, they weigh both rabbits. What variable are the students testing in their experiment?

A   how much water the rabbits receive

B   what kind of food the rabbits eat

C   how long the rabbits sleep

D   what kind of bedding the rabbits have

S4.B.1.1.4
Use the picture to the right to answer question 7.

7. The picture shows carrot roots. How do roots help a carrot meets its needs?

A   They produce food through photosynthesis.

B   They absorb water and nutrients from the soil.

C   They produce lovely flowers.

D   They keep away insects and other pests.

S4.B.1.1.5

8. Which group of pictures shows an insect that does **NOT** completely change its form to become an adult?

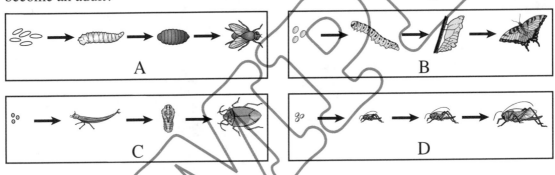

S4.D.2.1.1

9. Scientists have observed that different types of clouds are often associated with specific weather conditions.

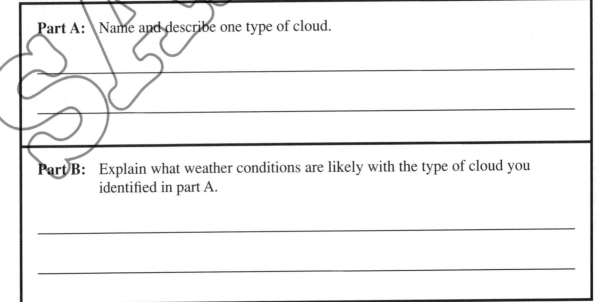

Part A: Name and describe one type of cloud.

_____

_____

Part B: Explain what weather conditions are likely with the type of cloud you identified in part A.

_____

_____

S4.B.3.3.2

Use the pictures below to answer question 10.

Farmers plant cotton seeds.	Farmers fertilize the soil and water the plants.	Farmers harvest the plants.	Farmers separate the cotton fibers from the plants and seeds.	The cotton fibers are twisted into threads.

10. Which conclusion can be drawn from this chart?

    A   People grow plant fibers to meet their clothing needs.

    B   People depend on the natural environment to grow food.

    C   People compete with pests for Earth's limited resources.

    D   People are threatening the environment with global warming.

S4.C.1.1.2

Use the list below to answer question 11.

List of Objects
- gold watch
- plastic toy
- wooden ruler
- rubber ball
- steel fork

11. Students in a science class are given this list of objects to classify. Which physical characteristic can **best** be used to classify all these objects together in the same group?

    A   shape

    B   magnetism

    C   state of matter

    D   ability to conduct electricity

S4.C.1.1.1

Use the chart below to answer question 12.

Good Conductors of Heat	Poor Conductors of Heat
Silver spoon	Plastic fork
Copper pan	Glass jar
Iron nail	

12. The chart shows objects that are good and poor conductors of heat. Which object belongs in the empty space on the chart?

    A   copper wire

    B   aluminum pot

    C   rubber glove

    D   iron griddle

S4.B.3.3.1, S4.B.3.3.5

13. Communities depend on the natural environment for everyday human activities.

Part A: Describe one way people in your community depend on their natural environment.

_____

_____

Part B: Describe one way your community is affected by pollution.

_____

_____

S4.D.1.2.2

Use the chart below to answer question 14.

Nonrenewable Products	Reusable Products
Oil	Bricks
Natural gas	

14. Which product belongs in the blank space on the chart?

A   drinking water

B   coal

C   chocolate candy

D   clothing

S4.B.2.1.1

15. A cactus is a plant that lives in the desert. Why are the roots of the cactus close to the surface of the ground?

A   They help the cactus to stay warm.

B   They produce oxygen for the cactus.

C   They help the cactus to quickly absorb scarce rainwater.

D   They make food from sunlight.

S4.C.3.1.1

16. A special screwdriver can attract a screw just by coming very close to it. What force causes the screw to move?

A   push-and-pull force

B   gravity

C   magnetic force

D   friction

S4.A.2.2.1

Use the picture below to answer question 17.

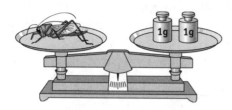

17. What is the mass of the insect on this balance?

   A   1 gram

   B   2 grams

   C   3 grams

   D   4 grams

S4.D.1.3.2

Use the diagram below to answer question 18.

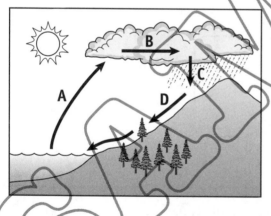

18. Which part of the diagram shows water in the process of evaporating?

   A   (A)

   B   (B)

   C   (C)

   D   (D)

S4.D.3.1.2

19. How long does it take Earth to complete one orbit around the sun?

   A   one day

   B   one week

   C   one month

   D   one year

S4.A.2.2.1

20. Which two tools are needed to measure the length and mass of this block of wood?

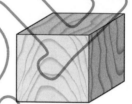

   A   a timer and a ruler

   B   a beaker and a thermometer

   C   a ruler and a balance

   D   a thermometer and a meter stick

S4.B.2.1.2

21. A rose bush has thorns. How do these thorns help the rose bush to survive in a grassland environment?

   A   They help the bush to get moisture.

   B   They anchor the bush to the ground.

   C   They protect the bush from animals that might eat it.

   D   They support the bush's stems and branches.

S4.A.2.2.1

22. What temperature is indicated on the thermometer to the right?

   A   9°C

   B   20°C

   C   15°C

   D   25°C

S4.D.2.1.3

23. Which weather instrument is used to measure air pressure?

   A   a barometer

   B   an anemometer

   C   a thermometer

   D   a rain gauge

S4.A.1.3.3

24. Water in a pot is heated on the stove. What will happen to the water when the temperature of the water in the pot reaches 100°C (212°F)?

   A   It will start to turn into a gas.

   B   It will start to become a solid.

   C   It will increase in mass.

   D   It will increase in weight.

Use the diagram below to answer question 25.

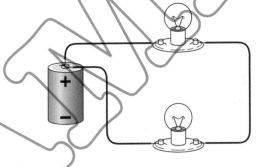

S4.C.2.1.1, S4.C.2.1.2

25.

Part A: Identify one form of energy that exists in this system.

_____

Part B: Describe how energy in this system changes its form.

_____

_____

S4.B.2.2.1

26. Which is a physical characteristic that Johnny inherits from his parents?

A   enjoying music

B   reading spy novels

C   eating an early breakfast

D   attached ear lobes

S4.A.3.1.1

27. Which is an example of a human-made system?

A   the living and nonliving parts of a lake

B   the roots, stem and leaves of a plant

C   the mouth, stomach and intestines of a giraffe

D   a battery and an electric light bulb connected by wires

S4.A.2.1.2

28. A scientist conducts an experiment to see if the number of flowers on a bush will increase if the bush has more water. The scientist has ten rose bushes. What variable should she change to investigate the question?

A   the age of the bushes

B   the temperature of the water

C   the amount of water they receive

D   the hours of sunlight they receive

Use the table below to answer question 29.

Month	Temperature	Month	Temperature	Month	Temperature
January	0°C	May	15°C	September	18°C
February	1°C	June	20°C	October	13°C
March	3°C	July	23°C	November	7°C
April	?	August	22°C	December	1°C

S4.A.2.1.3

29. The table shows the average monthly temperatures in Pittsburgh for one year. What is the best prediction for the average temperature in Pittsburgh in April?

A   1°C

B   10°C

C   16°C

D   20°C

S4.A.3.2.1

30. Scientists often use different models. A map is one type of model. It can be used to show the physical features of an area

---

Part A: Identify one other type of model.

_____

Part B: Describe what the type of model you identified in part A might represent.

_____

_____

S4.A.2.1.1

31. A scientist plants ten corn seeds in sandy soil and ten corn seeds in clay soil. He gives all the plants the same amount of water and sunlight. What question is the scientist trying to answer?

  A   How much soil and water do corn seeds need to grow?

  B   Do corn plants grow better in sandy or clay soil?

  C   Do corn plants grown in sandy soil need more water than corn plants grown in clay soil?

  D   What effect do soil and water have on the growth of corn plants?

S4.C.2.1.2

32. When a light bulb is turned on, energy changes from one form to another. Which best describes this change?

  A   Sound energy changes to light energy.

  B   Sound energy changes to electrical energy.

  C   Electrical energy changes to light energy.

  D   Magnetic energy changes to light energy.

S4.A.1.1.1

33. Which statement would be considered a scientific fact?

  A   Globes are the best models to represent planet Earth.

  B   Our universe will end one day in the near future.

  C   To make water boil, it must be heated to 100°C (212°F).

  D   The moon is the most beautiful object in the night sky.

Use the illustration below to answer question 34.

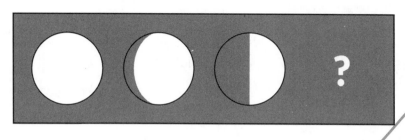

S4.A.3.3.2

34. Which phase of the moon is most likely to appear next?

A

B

C

D

S4.D.3.1.3

35. The diagram on the right shows Earth's orbit around the sun. The Northern Hemisphere is at its greatest tilt away from the sun. What season is it in Pennsylvania?

A   fall

B   winter

C   spring

D   summer

S4.A.2.1.1

36. A student places a plastic button on a table 1 inch from a strong magnet. The student observes if the button moves. The student removes the button and places a paper clip 1 inch from the magnet. The student observes whether the paper clip moves. Which question is the student trying to answer?

A   Is magnetism caused by gravity?

B   Which materials are magnetic?

C   Can a magnet work underwater?

D   Does light affect the power of a magnet?

S4.A.3.2.3

37. In a pond ecosystem, plants provide food and oxygen. Animals produce carbon dioxide and their wastes provide nutrients for plants. What would be the best type of model to study how this system works?

A   a diorama

B   a concept map

C   a terrarium

D   a globe

Use the diagrams below to answer question 38.

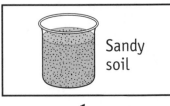
Sandy soil

1

Soil with high clay content

2

Soil with high content of decayed plant material

3

S4.A.2.1.1

38. Students collected samples of three different types of soils shown above. They inspected the three samples with a hand lens and rubbed each sample with their hands. Which question was their investigation designed to answer?

    A   How well does each type of soil support life?

    B   How well does each type of soil hold water?

    C   What is the texture of each type of soil?

    D   Which microscopic bacteria live in the soil?

S4.A.2.1.2

39. Two students wanted to find out which toy truck would move the farthest. They decided to let each truck roll down a ramp. Then they measured how far each toy truck rolled on the ground. Which of these should be held constant if they want a fair test?

    A   the height of the ramp

    B   the time of day

    C   the temperature of the room

    D   the weight of the ramp

S4.A.2.1.4

40. A fourth grade class recorded the high and low temperatures each day for five days. They created a table of their results. On which day of the week did the temperature change the most?

    A   Monday

    B   Wednesday

    C   Thursday

    D   Friday

TEMPERATURE READINGS

	Low Temperature (°C)	High Temperature (°C)
Monday	19	28
Tuesday	20	27
Wednesday	20	28
Thursday	18	26
Friday	19	29

S4.A.1.3.3

41. A student drew a line around the center of a balloon and measured its length. Then the student heated the balloon and measured the line every two minutes. The results are recorded in the chart to the right. What conclusion can be drawn from these results?

A   The warmer the balloon gets, the larger it becomes.

B   The balloon is unaffected by changes in temperature.

C   The balloon is larger in the freezer than outdoors.

D   The warmer the balloon gets, the smaller it becomes.

HOW TEMPERATURE AFFECTS AIR IN A BALLOON

Conditions of Balloon	Length of Line Around Balloon (in centimeters)
Balloon after coming out of the freezer	14 cm
Balloon at room temperature	21 cm
Balloon after being warmed for 2 min.	33 cm
Balloon after being warmed for 4 min.	54 cm

S4.A.1.1.2

42. Plastic wrap and other new packaging materials have greatly affected the environment.

Part A: Identify one other technological change that has affected the environment.

_____

Part B: Describe the impact on the environment of the change you identified in part A.

_____

_____

S4.D.1.3.3

43. How does a stream differ from a pond?

A   A stream has fish.   B   A stream has flowing water.

C   A stream has fresh water   D   A stream is large in size.

S4.A.2.2.1

44. Which instrument can be used to measure weight?

A

B

C

D

Use the graph below to answer question 45.

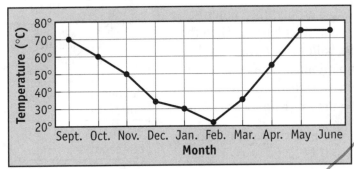

S4.A.2.1.4

45. A class recorded the outdoor temperature at noon on the first day of each month. They created the graph above with their results. What happened to the outdoor temperature from November to February?

A   It decreased.

B   It remained the same.

C   It increased.

D   It increased, then decreased.

S4.A.2.2.1

46. What is this instrument used for?

A   to measure changes in temperature

B   to measure the amount of rainfall

C   to see distant objects

D   to magnify small objects

S4.A.3.2.3

47. Which would be the best model to show the sun's energy warming Earth?

A   a pot of water boiling

B   a large lamp giving off heat

C   an oven baking bread

D   a spoon stirring hot soup

S4.A.2.1.4

48. What statement is a correct conclusion about the information in the graph?

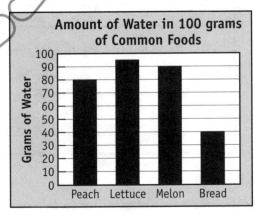

A   A peach contains less water than a lettuce of the same weight.

B   Lettuce contains less water than bread.

C   A melon contains more water than lettuce of the same weight.

D   Bread contains more water than a peach.

Use the chart below to answer question 49.

Day of the Week	Air Pressure (mm of mercury)	Weather Conditions
Monday	767	Fair, mild temperatures
Tuesday	767	Fair, mild temperatures
Wednesday	765	Cloudy, mild temperatures
Thursday	756	Rainy, windy, cool temperatures
Friday	754	Rainy, cool temperatures
Saturday	760	Fair, mild temperatures
Sunday	765	Sunny, mild temperatures

S4.D.2.1.2

49. Based on the chart, what kind of weather is most closely connected to falling air pressure?

    A   sunny   B   fair

    C   rainy   D   mild

Use the table below to answer question 50.

Solution	Time
50 mL water	45 minutes
50 mL water and 5 g salt	70 minutes
50 ml water and 10 g salt	120 minutes

S4.A.2.1.4

50. The table shows the time it took different solutions of water mixed with salt to freeze. What conclusion can be drawn from the information in this table?

    A   Freezing rates were the same for all three solutions.

    B   Water with more salt takes longer to freeze.

    C   Water with less salt takes longer to freeze.

    D   Salt dissolves more quickly in small amounts of water.

S4.A.1.3.4

51. If a fire destroys a forest, what is **most likely** to happen to the birds in that forest?

    A   They will migrate to a nearby forest.

    B   They will become herbivores.

    C   They will live in the ashes.

    D   They will learn to live in ponds, lakes, and streams.

S4.A.1.1.2

52. How do some kinds of packaging materials endanger the environment?

    A   They keep foods fresh.

    B   They use renewable products such as paper.

    C   They provide jobs to workers.

    D   They produce unnecessary solid waste.

S4.A.3.1.3

53. Which is an example of a nonliving part of a tropical rainforest ecosystem?

    A   an overhead canopy of tree leaves

    B   worms and other insects in the soil

    C   sunlight carrying energy to plants

    D   butterflies and other rainforest insects

S4.A.3.1.2

54. Why do animals living in a terrarium like this one need air?

    A   They need carbon dioxide for photosynthesis.

    B   They need water vapor for drinking.

    C   They need oxygen for respiration.

    D   They need sunlight for energy.

S4.D.1.1.1

55. Which best describes how the Appalachian Mountains were formed?

    A   Volcanoes brought lava to Earth's surface.

    B   Layers of sand and mud built up new rock.

    C   Sections of Earth's crust folded upwards.

    D   Glaciers created massive piles of debris.

S4.C.3.1.3

56. Which statement describes the location of the tree?

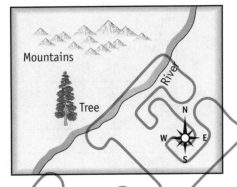

    A   east of the river

    B   south of the mountains

    C   south of the river

    D   east of the mountains

S4.C.2.1.4

57. Which characteristic of sound is affected when sound vibrations become more frequent?

    A   the loudness of the sound

    B   its reflection off a wall

    C   the pitch of the sound

    D   speed at which the sound travels

S4.D.1.2.3

58. What is one way that humans benefit from the use of water resources?

    A   They use water to irrigate crops in fields.

    B   They spread diseases by polluting lakes and rivers.

    C   They slow down groundwater recharge by pumping water from wells.

    D   They destroy wildlife by introducing species such as zebra mussels.

S4.C.1.1.1

59. Students in science class are investigating an unknown piece of matter. The piece of matter is solid, hard, and shiny. It is a good conductor of heat and electricity. It can also be attracted to a magnet. What could this matter be?

A   wood

B   iron

C   ice

D   glass

Use the drawing of the circuit below to answer question 60.

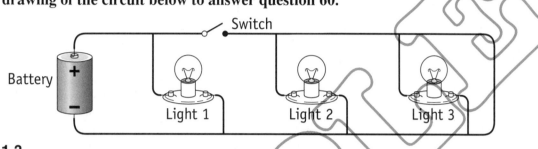

S4.C.2.1.3

60. Which light bulbs in the circuit will stay on when the switch is open?

A   none

B   light 1

C   lights 2 and 3

D   lights 1, 2 and 3

Use the diagram below to answer question 61.

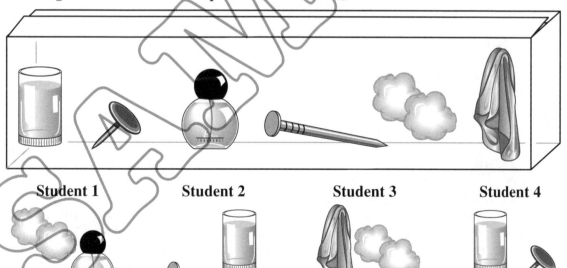

Student 1   Student 2   Student 3   Student 4

S4.C.1.1.2

61. A teacher had a box of objects. Each student was asked to form a group of two objects with common characteristics. Which student has made a group based on texture?

A   student 1

B   student 2

C   student 3

D   student 4

INDEX